S0-AYF-676

Edited by Alberic Stacpoole OSB
with Geoffrey and Jill Pinnock

Mary in Doctrine and Devotion

PAPERS OF THE LIVERPOOL CONGRESS, 1989,
OF THE ECUMENICAL SOCIETY OF
THE BLESSED VIRGIN MARY

THE LITURGICAL PRESS
Collegeville, Minnesota 56321

\# 25386103

BT
595
·E23
1989

THE LITURGICAL PRESS
Collegeville, Minnesota 56321

First edition 1990
Cover by Bill Bolger
Origination by The Columba Press
Printed in Ireland by
Genprint Limited, Dublin

ISBN 0-8146-1983-5

Copyright © 1990, The Columba Press and the Contributors

Contents

HOLY LIBRARY
CABRINI COLLEGE, RADNOR, PA.
0265

Dedicated to

Basil Christopher Butler, 1902 - 1986

Scholar and Deacon of the Church of England
Monk and Abbot of Downside, and Priest

Auxiliary to the Cardinal Archbishop of Westminster
who, at the Second Vatican Council,
championed Mary and ecumenism,
speaking especially for Anglicans,
who afterwards chaired or assiduously attended
all Anglican/Roman Catholic conversations

Introduction

Alberic Stacpoole, OSB
Roman Catholic, St Benet's Hall, Oxford

Within this decade (1979-89) five International Congresses of the Ecumenical Society of the Blessed Virgin Mary (ESBVM) have been held at Westminster, at Canterbury, in Dublin, in Chichester and lastly in Liverpool. Chichester had felicitously provided us with a 'two-cathedral' model, with an Anglican Theological College on the brink of celebrating the 150th anniversary of its foundation, with two outstandingly ecumenical bishops (the Anglican, our Co-Chairman, the Catholic, Co-Chairman of ARCIC II), and with a strong local branch, the West Sussex.

Liverpool has given us as much again. The great Gilbert Scott Anglican Cathedral was built by a Catholic architect; the new Metropolitan Cathedral of Christ the King was built by an Anglican[1] – and they are connected felicitously by Hope Street. Each has layers of meaning for the other. Cardinal Hume, giving his own witness to the reception of Pope John Paul II at Liverpool in June 1982, had this to say, 'As we approached the Anglican Cathedral, the crowds were greater and thicker than in any part of the route throughout the visit. But when we entered into that Cathedral, where the Pope was to remain but ten minutes or so, the response was electric, the clapping prolonged, the affection genuine, with happiness on every face. People let the tears run unabashed and in a totally unselfconcious manner. For my part, that moment in the Cathedral at Liverpool was a great cry for Christian unity on the part of thousands of people who had crammed into that great building.' We too had our unifying ecstasy in that great church, but in a lesser way, quietly (as befits the Marian mode), in the Lady chapel, free-standing and elegant – a miniature of the cathedral choir. Led not by Pope or bishop but by the Moderator of the Free Church Federal Council,[2] a Methodist who presided according to the Methodist eucharistic rite, with Methodist concelebrants, we were gathered, though small in numbers perhaps, into a wider ecclesial fellowship.

The Moderator, the Revd Dr John Newton, exercises his apostolate among the Methodists of Liverpool; and this was a great good fortune, for he and his fellow ministers and lay helpers gave such a strong lead at Congress that, by common accord, it was judged the first in which Methodism had predominated among the traditions: blessedly, if such judgment can in fact be made, 'it was their Congress'. (And if names are to be mentioned, we should record two others too: Rev Gerald Tedcastle and Rev Norman Wallwork, Liverpool secretary and Liturgical secretary to our Society).

The Congress was housed up on the hill at Christ's & Notre Dame College, Woolton, half a mile away from the home of Archbishop Derek Worlock, whose wide interests, especially in the apostolate of the laity, included our Society.[3] On the first evening he and his confrere, the Anglican Bishop David Sheppard,[4] dined with us and each gave their witness to ecumenism in this difficult city, divided by poverty, neglect and spiritual prejudice; united by adversity. These two prelates have just won the Collins biennial Religious Book Award (of £2000) for their joint authorship of *Better Together: Christian partnership in a hurt city* (Penguin 1989, 318p), an edition with a postscript on 'The soul of the nation' (289-306p). There, pursuing the Communion of Saints, they write, 'If a place can be identified with one particular denomination, so can devotion to the saints. Until recently this applied more sharply to Mary, the Mother of Jesus, than to any other whose memory we may encounter on the inward journey of life's pilgrimage. Hopefully, as we may see today from the membership of the Ecumenical Society of the Blessed Virgin Mary, even this centuries old misunderstanding is closer to being resolved.'(p 277). The two bishops devote a pair of consecutive chapters of their joint book to ecumenism, IV. Meeting-Point and V. Call to Partnership (61-113p).

Where Chichester had been a 'two-cathedral' Congress in 1986, Liverpool in 1989 became in fact a 'three-cathedral' Congress. On the penultimate day the whole congress of folk motored out into North Wales, past the Jesuit retreat centre of St Beuno's, to one of the oldest churches in Wales, the Cathedral of St Asaph. The highlight of this visit, breaking the course of study, was the episcopal Eucharist in the Anglican Church in Wales rite, presided over by Bishop Alwyn Rice Jones; and with him the Dean, Raymond Renowden, (whose 1965 monograph is entitled *The idea of unity*, and who went on to write in 1974 *The role of a cathedral today and tomorrow*). We felt that they were well prepared for such an occasion !

It would be well here to discuss our eucharistic practice at these Congresses. Our conventual eucharist was customarily held each midday, a different denomination leading on each occasion. On the Wednesday, the Methodists led in the Anglican cathedral ... and on the final day Archbishop Derek Worlock presided in the crypt chapel of his own cathedral. The Thursday was in fact different. Eastern Church lectures were given throughout the morning; and the day ended with Orthodox Vespers presided over by Bishop Kallistos of Diokleia. The reason for that choice of evening prayer is that the Orthodox eucharist is enormously ('inordinately' would be an uncomprehending criticism) long by western usage; and in the Orthodox liturgy there is a certain *disciplina arcana* in effect over against those who are not of that tradition – if one is not in communion with their bishop, one is not wholly welcome at their eucharist, and *a fortiori* as a communicant (whatever Catholicism may recognise as acceptably valid.[5]

The programme deliberately made no direct allowance for those who were unable to communicate in their tradition at their conventual eucharist. The custom of the members of ARCIC I and now ARCIC II (as we are told by our members, Bishop Edward Knapp-Fisher and Dr Edward Yarnold SJ) tends towards 'eucharistic fasting' on 'off' days, so that those who come together to build new bridges may feel the sorrow of separation as the structure is planned out. On Anglican days, Catholics 'starve' eucharistically; and on Catholic days Anglicans 'starve' – as witness of division unhealed, unity unestablished.

St Benedict, in his Rule, tells us that the life of a monk should be always lenten 'but since monks cannot be convinced of this ...' Our various eucharistic communities were unconvinced, and so we held extra-curricular eucharists before breakfast on non-Anglican or non-Roman days of conventual celebration accordingly. As to the Catholics (and I speak as a participant), on the Wednesday Canon John McHugh led us with six celebrants in the main College chapel. On the Thursday, Fr William McLoughlin OSM (Servite) led with eight concelebrants and two deacons, one singing the gospel. On the Friday Bishop Mervyn Alexander of Clifton, our RC Executive Co-Chairman, led with eight concelebrants and two deacons, and again the gospel was sung. By then a congregation of some forty-five had gathered: I record this to show how much our 'unofficial' eucharists in their own denomination are valued, and how little 'eucharistic starvation' appeals !

On two of these days – the third being taken up with the St Asaph's Eucharist – a group of Anglicans led by Bishop Knapp-Fisher held their own pre-prandial Eucharist in a small neighbouring chapel, with a congregation that likewise increased on the second occasion. In close proximity, virtually the same Prayer of Thanksgiving and certainly the same scriptural readings for the Liturgy of the Word were used in each chapel at the same approximate time, by gatherings so close to one another in more than one way. On reflection, this provoked among our Council members the feeling that an established (from 1968) and trusted ecumenical society should take a more advanced position in the matter.

There are precedents indeed, one involving the Apostolic Delegate (Mgr Cardinale)[6] and the Bishop of Willesden (Rt Revd Graham

Leonard)[7], for uniting the first part of the Mass, viz. the liturgy of the Word of God to include the Creed[8]; and then separating communities for the sacramental liturgy, both apart but in awareness of blessing and dismissal. Bishop Knapp-Fisher, author of a recent study, *Eucharist: many-sided mystery*, was asked by the Society's officers to discover the state of opinion and make proposals. Opinion proved divided, in some cases vehemently; the proposal was to put a practical scheme before the October Council at Westminster.

At Council the debate waxed and waned. It was finally felt that such a course would need virtually unanimous assent among us (not forthcoming); and that, while we should wisely innovate, at the same time we should take the same care as our forebears to guard the respect that has built up for the prudence of our activities. While nothing may be so important as the Eucharist – and therefore its conduct among us – we are nevertheless gathered to further another issue, mariology/marian devotion. We should keep our powder dry for issues in that quarter.

This can be viewed pessimistically. But ARCIC members came to find such events as a particular kind of blessing. At the time of their fasting they would always make a 'spiritual communion'; and thus what began as a renunciation (i.e. a negative experience) became a positive experience in another realm of the gifts of the spirit. ARCIC members – alternate ones on alternate days – felt challenged to a higher subjective degree of sharing with their brothers and sisters of the other tradition, that is, to a closer bond not directly aided by the grace that flows from receiving the great sacrament of unification. That one group should receive the sacramental reality, the other the spiritual; and then the one receive the spiritual, the other the sacramental, brought both groups to an experiential bond debatably closer than that of both receiving the fulness of the sacrament on all occasions.

It may be noticed that 'eucharistic starvation' also carries another connotation. When Christians are undergoing a conversion process from one tradition to another, or when baptised (and confirmed?) catechumens are preparing perhaps for Easter vigil communion, there is an advent or lenten period of expectancy that may be expressed as deliberate eucharistic starvation or forebearance from the sacrament. And further, the custom of coming up for a blessing at the moment of communion is becoming prevalent. He or she who subscribes to another ecclesial communion/tradition/Church, who is obedient to another bishop or moderator or presiding minister, cannot share the same bond in word and sacrament with everyone else. Yet people may offer themselves not as full eucharistic fellows but as fellow-seekers, their hands not outstretched to receive but crossed at their breast to experience. They come at the communion time to be blessed with the blessing of a God shared. Such a blessing recalls the Orthodox tradition that outsiders may come not for the consecrated host but for solemnly blessed bread, a sign of the Sign. It is not the fulfilment, but it is half way to the house; and it is a kind of eucharistic hospitality which is able to be offered both ways within the divided circumstances of our age.

We should reiterate our policy of conduct in ESBVM, because it wells up from our long and joyous experience. Slogans often give the signal best, and can be 'unpacked' if not understood.[9] In the work of the Society we try to achieve a balance between these three, all most valuable in their right and place: *say–pray–play*. In all our various events, whether at local branch or international levels, we try each time to elicit at least two of these. At the Congress, the first was expressed in the seven main sessions where, in seventy minutes, a paper was read and discussed; and the two periods of Communications when some fifteen short addresses were given by members less expert or with simpler things to say.

As to prayer, besides the conventual eucharists there was a morning Office at 09.15 and an evening Office at about 21.45 (texts tried and set for all our congresses). There was also an element of what monks call *lectio divina*, or prayerful study/studying prayer in the various addresses. As to play, we toured the Liverpool Cathedrals with guides, visited Speke Hall, had a tea and talk on Lourdes from Dom Martin Haigh at St Austin's Church, Grassendale, and were delighted by a lecture-recital by Dr Mary Remnant.[10] She brought her ancient instruments from another world,[11] and with slides also, she told us of '*Pilgrims and music on the way to Walsingham*' (the historic Marian shrine and pilgrim centre on the Norfolk coast). And there was a celebratory dinner, with fifteen speeches given by those from Washington to Canada, from Sweden to Switzerland, Dublin to Belfast, Scotland to Wales, Yorkshire to Liverpool – with a word from Rome. This has become a way of showing ourselves at least that we really are an international gathering. At the end of it all, one participant wrote, 'I did appreciate the feast of good things prepared for us in Liverpool: by the end I felt like a small glass jug into which an attempt was being made to pour the whole ocean !'

At the outset there were blessings from those who looked to us to succeed in our Society. The Apostolic Pro-Nuncio wrote from London, 'It can be taken that the sentiments expressed by His Eminence Cardinal Willebrands would be a suffcient assurance of the Holy Father's concern and interest', he having sent a blessing in other years. Writing from the *Secretariatus ad Christianorum Unitatem Foven-*

dam of which he is President, Cardinal Johannes Willebrands said, 'It is my privilege and pleasure to offer my greetings and warm good wishes ... In choosing the theme *Mary in Theology & Devotion* you will be building on a growing convergence among Christians in their understanding of the role of Mary in the mystery of salvation. Be assured that, in your shared prayer and reflection, you will be contributing importantly to the realisation of that unity which we know to be the will of Christ for his followers ...'

What follows, written on 2 March this year, has a poignancy enormously enhanced by Mikhail Gorbachev's visit to the Holy Father on 1 December, when a new *Perestroika* pervaded their Slav-to-Slav concord and hope for the future. Referring to the Pope's encyclical *Redemptoris Mater* (Assumption 1987), the Cardinal said: 'Pope John Paul stressed how deeply the Catholic Church and the Churches of the East feel united in their love and praise for the Mother of God, Theotokos. He also affirmed the growing agreement between the Catholic Church and the other Churches and ecclesial communities of the West on fundamental matters of faith, including matters relating to the Virgin Mary. The growth in sympathy and in shared understanding with which Christians have been graced in recent years must not be underestimated. The continuance and the deepening of this process is a priority for the Catholic Church, as Pope John Paul never ceases to recall.' A blessing followed. This message is amazingly resonant of what must have been occurring in those months (not to say years, as Cardinal Casaroli well remembers) leading to that portentous meeting which melted the ice for the Church Universal and the Soviet empire, promising the beginnings of a re-union.

Archbishop Robert Runcie, our Co-President, sent his message – thoughtfully by hand of a participant. 'I was interested to learn that your theme is to be *Mary in Theology & Devotion*. One of the perennial tensions within the Christian Church is that between devotion and spirituality on the one hand, and theology on the other. This can be exemplified in the history of Marian devotion and teaching. The ecumenical movement, and the Ecumenical Society of the Blessed Virgin Mary in particular, has made a significant attempt to hold these two aspects together. It has grounded right devotion to Mary in a sound ecclesiology centred upon the Incarnation and Atonement of Jesus Christ. I wish you well for your Congress and will remember it in my prayers.' The other Co-President, Cardinal Basil Hume, also sent us a prayer of blessing, 'May the Mother of God intercede for us so that we may move ever more closely in full Communion'.

As to our Patrons, two were present (Dr Newton and Bishop

Kallistos), Cardinal Suenens promised us his prayers, and Bishop Graham Leonard of London sent us this signal, 'The theme is timely, reflecting as it does both the unique insight which Mary gives us for a true understanding of the Incarnation, and the example which she constantly provides of the way in which we should respond to the divine initiative. It is only through the unity of Divine grace and the human response of obedience, of which Mary is the embodiment, that the will of God both for the Church and for all mankind can be fulfilled. May God bless you so that through your worship, study and fellowship, you may grow in your love of God and in your love for one another, to the glory of the Blessed Trinity.' This was especially appreciated.

Of our three Executive Co-Chairmen, one was present among us (Bishop Mervyn Alexander of Clifton), Dr Gordon Wakefield sent good wishes through the Methodist grapevine, and Bishop Eric Kemp of Chichester sent us the following, 'Greetings from Chichester with happy recollections of the last [1986] Congress in Chichester, and prayers that the Liverpool Congress may be equally successful. Please convey to the Society our grateful thanks from Chichester for the gift of the statue of Our Lady [in the Lady chapel] by John Skelton, which is much admired, as a valuable addition to the many works of modern art for which the Cathedral is already distinguished.[12] It is very good to see the ecumenical spread of the Liverpool papers – which illustrates the way in which Martin Gillett's [13] original vision has been translated into reality.'

Other letters and signals of warm encouragement came from former speakers both sides of 'The Pond', for example from Mrs Mary Ann De Trana, an Orthodox from Richmond, Virginia (cf Chichester papers). From Florida one of our oldest allies, Dr Ross Mackenzie, cabled on the opening day, 'Christ is risen and Mary brings us together to pray. So blessings on you all in your deliberations.' Mgr Murphy of the National Shrine, Washington DC, had been coming, but eventually sent a blessing.

Bishop Kemp commended the ecumenical spread of the papers offered. Our custom is to arrange that the four ecumenical aspects of Christendom are in some way represented. Beside the papers published in this volume, Anglican contributions came from Rev William S Bridcut (Church of Ireland), 'To Jesus through Mary', and Mrs Joan Ashton,[14] 'Russia in the light of Marian prophecy'.[15] Among the Catholic papers published here, Canon John McHugh continues an earlier argument from Chichester 1986 and Hengrave Hall 1988;[16] and Sister Lutgart Govaert gave us our reserve paper, having been called to Jerusalem, on Newman's Mariology.[17] Other Catholic contributions were made by a Franciscan Friar of the

Atonement, Fr Michael Seed (ecumenical adviser to Cardinal Hume) on 'Devotion to our Lady of the Atonement'; and, from the Dublin Institute of Technology, Domhnall Ó Sioradáin on 'Mary, Queen of Ireland: Mary's place in the history of the Irish Church'.[18] Of the communications not committed to record, a word should be said. It often happens that those best delivered or most suitably given in person *ex corde* are too personal or charmingly done to be put to paper, like a butterfly on cork. Instances of this were Patricia, Countess Michaelowska, with her, 'Mary, a real woman'; or Rev John Richards, 'Matthew's Mary & her "Yes."'

Sometimes Communications are used to further the Society's policy, as at Chichester, when the late Margaret Kneebone gave us her last 'Thoughts on the future development of ESBVM'. On this occasion Rev Dr Ronald Gibbins, chairman of the London branch, offered us 'A Free Church evaluation of ESBVM'. He had this to say, 'Marian theology has been controversial for Protestant Christians for a long time. One of the aims of our Society is to encourage and enable all Christians to grow together in worship and service of the Lord. It has been difficult for some of our [Free Church] members, who belong to the reformed tradition yet are sympathetic with our aims, to reconcile their membership with their own Church loyalties ... Most Free Church Christians are by tradition and faith not really tuned to Marian faith and devotion. Those of us who have become members of ESBVM have made a venture of faith; and we look to our Society to help in creating dialogue with Christians whose tradition does not include devotion to Our Lady, or recognition of her place in the communion of saints. I would suggest three ways in which the Society's members can help in this situation :

1. We should broaden the terms of study sessions to include more biblical study, especially from a critical point of view;

2. We should make a particular effort to bridge the gap existing between those who still believe that prayers addressed to Mary are made in error, because they believe that Catholics are thereby placing Mary in the Godhead, and the true teachings of the Catholic faith, which rightly regard Mary as the most important member of the communion of saints;

3. We should be more energetic in finding ways of dealing with misunderstandings and fears existing in the minds of our fellow Christians. Most of our ESVBM literature, fine as it is, reaches only our own members (which is talking to the converted) and is very intellectual. Perhaps we should prepare simpler literature about the place of Mary in our theology, commending her as an ecumenical sign to fellow Christians. We could also prepare simpler literature which would help Catholics to understand the difficulties faced by

Free Church Christians.'[19]

On the first evening, after our guests had dined with us, they gave us a remarkable triple insight into ecumenism. First Archbishop Derek Worlock talked of social ecumenism; then Bishop David Sheppard of spiritual ecumenism; then Dr John Newton of doctrinal ecumenism. What had been called 'a dynamic duo' has lately become a triple act. Mgr Worlock has been in Liverpool thirteen years, Bishop Sheppard twelve and Dr Newton not yet three; the last is joining a well-honed partnership, but has been accepted at once.

The partnership began with a Government department letter asking comments on its inner city study, which Church leaders chose to answer as one, showing that on social matters there were no differences between them. The shop stewards arrived under cover of darkness to ask for help, wanting to meet the management who would not meet them. They chose to march through the streets to draw attention to their plight; and the two bishops joined that march in the front rank – where the media went to ask what was occurring. After a while both management and shop stewards turned to the Church for wisdom and mediation, asking 'Can the Church do anything to help?' It was then that the Churches began worrying about unemployment, and attempted to create new jobs. The Church, being of the community, began to concern itself with housing and work, race relations and water crises – and that led on to the Church & Politics debate. Soon the journalists were asking, 'What about the Mersey miracle?' and then, 'What's all this about ecumenism?' The reply came, 'That means bishops are standing up for our jobs.' And more and more the two bishops were drawn together on social issues that became ecumenism.

Bishop Sheppard talked of the bitter division that has long been endemic in Liverpool, which grew worse as the Irish potato famine brought disaffected immigrants to the city at a time when the Tate sugar trading was bringing riches to the community. Mistrust set in: bully-boys used to clear out non-Catholics and fix local politics (in a way since familiar to Northern Ireland). Icons of the Pope or of King Billy would appear; and the possibility of harmonious mixed marriages receded. It was in 1979 that in a rough area, Kirby, the Churches joined together for Stations of the Cross on Good Friday. Gradually such religious habits were shared: unhurried Holy Week services, slide lectures upon Breughel's religious paintings, joint pilgrimages to Lindisfarne or Assisi or Iona. The young were glad of these, but then became impatient at ecclesial disciplines, until explained the processes and shown that holding to these disciplines had allowed them into a closer profundity together. They then met more often in prayer and devotion, bringing that into the context of mission – to serve 'a hurt situation' such as unemployment. Prayer brought the young into other commitments that were not merely secular, and gradually into a spiritual partnership.

Joint social and political action implies at least a rudimentary doctrinal agreement as to God's kingdom and the role of religious in society. Spiritual ecumenism will free the log-jams of doctrinal disagreement. In a memorable 1964 sermon, Archbishop Michael Ramsey suggested that there may be depths below the doctrinal where heart speaks to heart. He spoke of 'a similar apartness in the realm of thought and nearness in the depth of religious meaning in the case of some of the cleavages about faith, justification and the sacraments.' Dr John Newton agreed with Dr Ramsey that doctrinal questions may be illuminated by being set within our traditions of spirituality, a larger context of thought and experience. 'Heart speaks to heart ' (Newman's *Cor ad cor loquitur*) means an enrichment of ecumenical dialogue, not an evasion of difficulties. Dr Newton recorded that 'our own discussion of doctrine in the Church Leaders' Group has certainly been rooted in shared devotion and worship – in many public occasions among Churches, particularly at services for the inauguration of local covenants; in spending time together in Holy Week; and in shared prayer in the two bishops' chapels ... [which] enabled us to tackle serious doctrinal differences in a relaxed and free manner.'(See Appendix I below)

And what of those that got away, as fishermen say? At the planning stage we had many fond hopes, and sometimes it is well to display them as a sign of possibilities from the past (and for the future?). Rev Professor Donald G. Dawe, a loyal contributor down the years, chairman of the United States branch, a Presbyterian from Virginia, who at Chichester gave a report on 'Marian Devotions in the United States today' (*Mary and the Churches*, 169-71), wrote to us between Congresses: 'I would like to make good on the paper that I suggested for the last meeting, but was not in a position to complete. [He had to be away in Africa.] My concern would be to evaluate theologically the significance of the psychological interpretations of Mary and Marian devotion. My concern would not primarily be with those negative characterisations of Mary that have dominated so much of the psychological analysis of Marian devotion. Rather, my concern would be with those psychological interpreters who have taken a positive view of Mary. I have in mind particularly the tradition coming from Jung through Heiler to Victor White OP. There has been a new group of feminist writers of late who have been concerned with this positive psychological evaluation of Marian devotion as a support for their position. I believe this poses some important theological issues that I should like to introduce...' I offer this quotation from a long letter, to show how much thought goes into planning, which does not mature at the time. Perhaps this idea will issue in a more advanced paper for our proposed Winchester International Congress of 1991, DV.

And what of more such hopes on horizons? Fr Terence O'Brien SDB (cf *Mary and the Churches*, 158-63), who had offered a development of his Chichester Comunication, wrote six months before the Congress that he had been asked to go to Nairobi by the local Archbishop to lead the priests there in 'Growth to maturity'. He was left with no other course than to accept Nairobi and refuse Liverpool; we may rejoice in that our loss is Africa's gain, and their need is surely beyond ours. Fr Michael J. Lapierre SJ from Ontario offered a paper on 'The Mother of God in the life of Thomas Merton' (the American Cistercian); and that would have widened our set of speeches on the celebratory evening, had Fr Lapierre been able to carry it through. We asked Gerald Bonner of Durham University to present a paper, who was honoured by the invitation but unable to take it up through force of work; yet 'if at some future date you were to invite me to read a paper on Augustine's Mariology, I should be happy to accept.' (*vide* Winchester 1991). And other papers were lower on our horizon, particularly two on the Banneux Notre-Dame in Belgium, eight apparitions of the so-called 'Virgin of the Poor' in 1933.[20]

A last word should be said regretting that our Constitution and Publications Secretaries, Revd Geoffrey and Mrs Jill Pinnock, were not able to be present for the first time this decade. A fortnight earlier, on Sunday 12 March (as for the Annunciation on 25 March), Jill Pinnock had been done the honour of preaching the Oxford University Sermon in New College Chapel, upon the words of Luke: 'And Mary kept all these things and pondered them in her heart.' She pointed out that the anticipated feast was the Annunciation *of* the Lord *to* Our Lady. She ended with the formal invocation: 'May we, now and always, here in this College of St Mary Winton and everywhere, know the encouragement of her intercession, from whose virgin womb the Author of life itself was born ...' [21]

Fittingly, the Congress ended with a pontifical High Mass, celebrated by Archbishop Derek Worlock in his own Metropolitan Cathedral of Christ the King, in the Edwin Lutyens crypt chapel. Nearby is the Lady Chapel for the crypt (there being another in the new main church, with its own statue); and this includes the bronze statue of the Virgin and Child by David John. It was a peaceful thanksgiving Mass involving as much participation as possible, both by priests and by laity, by Catholics and their separated brethren. A collection had been made, as at Chichester, but where that Cathedral had a beautiful Lady Chapel awaiting a statue and had the tradition of Walter Hussey in its aisles (*note 12*), it was felt that this sometimes sad city had other needs. We agreed that our ESBVM Congress simply had to leave a remembrance, but one attuned to the work of the two bishops who had written together *Better Together*. So, at the moment of the presentation of the gifts, our Treasurer Ivan Kightley brought forward on a salver for formal presentation at the Mass by the Archbishop, our collected and consolidated cheque for £600 to be offered for the work of the Liverpool Churches Urban Development Fund.

Fond farewells followed: another Congress, another Eastertide – the next will be our ninth, at a rate of four a decade.

A last thought: it is a long and blessed journey from 1977, when that Congress collapsed for lack of interest – but it is God who giveth growth!

Notes

1. The late Sir Frederick Gibberd, architect and author of *The Metropolitan Cathedral of Christ the King. Liverpool.* (1968).

2. This office is held for a year, and not only by Methodists. That it was within our year some found fortunate and others confusing.

3. At the Second Vatican Council Mgr Worlock took a special interest in the apostolate of the laity. Because of this, he was appointed a Consultor to the Council of the Laity during 1967-76; and from 1977 he has been a member of the Pontifical Laity Council and Committee for the Family. In 1980 he became chairman of the National Pastoral Council at Liverpool, drafting the episcopal response, *The Easter People.* In my book, **Vatican II by those who were there** (Chapman 1986), by his choice he contributed a chapter entitled, 'Toil in the Lord: the laity in Vatican II'.

4. Ordained in 1955, he spent two years as assistant curate in Islington, then a dozen years as warden of the Mayflower Family Centre in Canning Town, E16. Consecrated a bishop in 1969, he served at Woolwich until he was transferred to Liverpool in 1975. He is the author of *Built as a City* (1974), *Bias to the poor* (1983) and the 1984 Richard Dimbleby Lecture, *The Other Britain.*

5. The state of the ecumenical debate on this most delicate subject is that one tradition may rightly declare aspects of another as indeed 'valid', but may not properly declare any as 'invalid' (but at most 'not proven valid') in their own regard. We may affirm the positive, but not impose the negative.

6. Archbishop Hyginus Eugene Cardinale, DD, JCD, (1916-83), Apostolic Delegate to the Bishops of England & Wales (1962-9); Apostolic Nuncio to Belgium, Luxembourg and the European Community (1969-83). He was one of the Society's first members, his influence counting enormously at that frail moment. Cf his celebrated lecture 'Pope Pius XII and the Blessed Virgin Mary', in Alberic Stacpoole, *Mary's Place in Christian Dialogue* (St Paul Publications, 1982), 248-60.

7. As Bishop Suffragan of Willesden (1964-73), he was a member of the Society. As Bishop of Truro (1973-81) he was in Cornwall when that branch of ESBVM was founded. As Bishop of London (1981-) he has become, after Cardinal Suenens, the second of our Patrons. (The others are Dr John Newton and Bishop Kallistos, the four representing four principal traditions).

8. Mgr Cardinale had been the first Catholic prelate to preach in an Anglican church, when, indeed at the invitation of Dr Leonard, he preached in St Mary Magdalene's, Munster Square, the two prelates jointly giving the final blessing.

9. In another orbit, I found myself seminar/tutoring a Special Subject at Oxford involving the Gallipoli Campaign. When all had disastrously gone wrong, the Asquith Cabinet sent out spies and inspectors, lastly Kitchener himself, to ask – in a word – 'stay, or away?' The only military brilliance was in the instant double withdrawal: perhaps there is a moral here?

10. After studying piano and violin at the RCM (Gold Medal), she took a Churchill travelling fellowship for research in eight European countries in 1967, and then took a DPhil in 1972 with a thesis on bowed instruments in medieval England. She now lectures at the RCM on the history of instruments. She had developed a series of lecture-recitals, given in Europe and America. She is the author of *Musical Instruments of the West* (Batsford 1978) and *English Bowed Instruments* (Clarendon 1986), her doctorate revised for publication.

11. Lyre, harp, psaltery, gittern, mandora, rebec, fiddle, organistrum, gemshorn, shawm, crumhorn, chimebells and others.

12. Walter Hussey was Dean of Chichester from 1955-77, and Dean Emeritus till his death in August 1985. From 1966 he was for eleven years chairman of the Diocesan Art Council. An Hon FRIBA, he had been a great collector of the work of young artists, before they were famous, for the churches of his concern: St Matthew, Northampton from 1937, etc. In music he commissioned works from Britten, Walton, Bliss; in art and craft from Graham Sutherland OM, John Piper, Geoffrey Clarke and Robert Potter. Cf his Pitkin Pictorial, *Chichester Cathedral* (1972).

13. Founder General Secretary, d. 1980. He was made KCSG in his last year.

14. This spring Harper and Row (San Francisco) has published the United States edition of her book, *Mother of all nations: the visitations of the Blessed Virgin Mary and her message for today,* 223pp, $9.95. The English edition of 1988 was from The Lamp Press, £2.99. Both carry a Foreword by the General Secretary of the ESBVM. It is an ecumenical book, open to the evidence coming from Catholic, Anglican, Protestant and Oriental sources (near east and far east both); not surprisingly, Protestant evidence is least abundant.

15. The twelve chapters given to locality of visions does not include Russia: this is new work, germane to the unfolding religious/political situation.

16. Kallistos of Diokleia, 'The sanctity and glory of the Mother of God', *The Way Supplement*: 'Mary in Christian Tradition', 51 (Autumn 1984), 79-96: subtitled 'Orthodox Approaches', it was delivered at the Dublin Congress of 1984. Bishop Kallistos and

Edward Yarnold SJ, 'The Immaculate Conception: a search for convergence', ESBVM Pamphlet Sept 1987, 11p. Cf *Mary and the Churches*, 13-15.

17. This subject was first aired among us by Stephen Dessain of the Birmingham Oratory, in an early ESBVM Pamphlet. At the 1979 Congress, Fr Roderick Strange (who had recently completed a DPhil dissertation on Newman, with Fr Dessain as his supervisor) delivered an allocution in the University Church of St Mary the Virgin, from Newman's pulpit, 'The development of Newman's Marian thought and devotion', *One in Christ* 1980–1/2. 114-26; ESBVM extract, 61-72. (These also contain an appreciation of Martin Gillett, KCSG, 1902-80).

18. Cf Céline Mangan OP, 'The Irish Joint Statement on Marian Devotion', in ESBVM Pamphlet 1985 (a Communication at the Dublin Congress, 1984).

19. Among our Society there is a constant debate as to the 'level' of our meetings and publications. The ESBVM Pamphlets which go out with the current Newsletter are deliberately varied in length and intellectual intensity. In a word, some are doctrinal, some devotional. We do not make strong distinctions between e.g. Catholics and Free Church, but speak and think with one ecumenical voice.

20. Cf Damien Walne and Joan Flory, 'The Virgin of the Poor: the apparitions at Banneux', CTS D544 (1983), 1-20; and Peggy Palmer, 'The Virgin of the Poor', Caritas Banneux ND, Georgian Heights, Route de Banneux, 19 Pilgrims Way, Canterbury CT1 1XU. Tours are offered to Banneux at £100.

21. A text is available.

APPENDIX I

Address by Dr John A Newton (Methodist),
Patron and President of the Eighth International Congress
at Liverpool during Easter Week 1989: 'Ecumenism'.

Speaking of discussion of doctrine in the Church Leaders' Group, a group which includes our other two Congress Patrons, Archbishop Worlock and Bishop David Sheppard, Dr Newton brought together an Anglican break-away and a Jesuit reunionist, in these words:

As far as our approach to doctrinal issues is concerned, I think we may have been unconsciously following John Wesley's ecumenical principles as discerned by Cardinal Bea SJ. (Rather like Molière's M. Jourdain, who exclaimed, 'Good heavens! I've been speaking prose for more than forty years without knowing it!') Cardinal Bea, as first President of the Vatican Secretariat for Promoting Christian Unity, wrote a Preface to Michael Hurley's 1968 re-issue of John Wesley's *Letter to a Roman Catholic*. Bea saw the *Letter* as anticipating by more than a century and a half 'many of the insights and ideals of the modern ecumenical movement.' Under this anticipation of a modern ecumenical approach, he distinguished the following principles:

a) The *Letter* stresses what Christians hold in common, before looking at the differences, and tries to see the differences themselves in the light of what is already held in common.

b) Wesley does not blink the serious differences he sees between Catholics and Protestants, but the thrust of the *Letter* is that things that unite them are more important – as fundamentals of the Faith – than those which divide them.

c) The *Letter* distinguishes between ecumenism, says Cardinal Bea, i.e. the promotion of Christian unity between those of different communions, and proselytising. Cf Wesley: 'My dear friend, consider: I am not persuading you to leave or change your religion, but to follow after that fear and love of God without which all religion is vain.'

d) It stresses that the given measure of unity, which separated Christians already enjoy, must be expressed in practical charity – in working together except where deep differences of conscientious conviction forbid it.

APPENDIX II

ECUMENICAL SOCIETY OF THE BLESSED VIRGIN MARY
ITS AIMS

ESBVM was established to advance the study at various levels of the place of the Blessed Virgin Mary in the Church, under Christ, and the related theological questions; and in the light of such study to promote ecumenical devotion.

'Instead of being a cause of division among us, Christian reflections on the role of the Virgin Mary should be a cause of rejoicing and a source of prayer' (Brother Max Thurian of Taizé). Mary's place in the Church should be given full consideration in ecumenical dialogue leading to Christian unity (cf *Lumen Gentium* VIII). Experience since the Vatican Council shows: Mary does not divide; she brings together.

The Society was called into being in 1967 by friends of several Christian traditions wishing to ensure that this vital element of religious experience was given its place in current dialogue, its aims being promoted at various pastoral levels, and theologians being asked always to play their part in providing sound teaching.

Membership is open to those who support these aims, all traditions and members being accorded equal respect. Annual subscriptions entirely support the Society, offering members entry to all meetings, a vote at deliberative meetings, and availability of all issued publications. There are now more than ten branches in England, others in Dublin, Washington DC, and Rome, and other members world-wide. The branches, as the Society at national level, give themselves in due measure to study, devotion and fellowship.

Write to Membership Secretary, 11 Belmont Road, Wallington, Surrey SM6 8TE.

Officers of the IXth International Congress,
Ecumenical Society of the Blessed Virgin Mary (ESBVM),
at Christ's & Notre Dame College, Liverpool.

PRESIDENTS
The Most Revd Dr Robert Runcie, PC, Archbishop of Canterbury†
Cardinal Basil Hume, OSB, Archbishop of Westminster †

PATRONS
Cardinal Léon-Josef Suenens, former Archbishop of Malines*
The Right Revd Dr Graham Leonard, PC, Bishop of London†
The Revd Dr John Newton,*
Moderator of the Free Church Federal Council
The Right Revd Kallistos, Bishop of Diokleia (Dr Ware)*

CO-CHAIRMEN
The Right Revd Dr Eric Kemp, Bishop of Chichester†
The Right Revd Mervyn Alexander, Bishop of Clifton*
The Revd Dr Gordon Wakefield

THE SOCIETY'S OFFICERS
Dom A J Stacpoole, OSB, MC, – General Secretary*
Revd Dr E J Yarnold, SJ, – Co-General Secretary*
Mr J P Farrelly, – Membership Secretary*
Mr I D Kightley, – Hon Treasurer*
Mr John Dunning,– Conference Treasurer*
Revd C N Wallwork, – Liturgy Secretary*
Revd & Mrs G Pinnock, – Constitution/Publications Secretaries
Revd W Burridge, WF, – Press Secretary*

OFFICERS OF THE LIVERPOOL COMMITTEE
Revd Gerald Tedcastle*
Mr Joe O'Connor*
Mrs Margaret McGinn*
Miss Celia Gallagher*

PATRONS OF THE LIVERPOOL CONGRESS
President: The Revd Dr John Newton,*
Moderator of the Free Church Federal Council
The Most Revd Derek Worlock, Archbishop of Liverpool*
The Right Revd David Sheppard, Bishop of Liverpool*

† *Sent a Blessing*
* *Present at the Congress*

The doctrine of the Immaculate Conception: reflections on a problem in ecumenical dialogue

Very Rev Canon John McHugh, DD, LsS, PhL.
Roman Catholic, Durham University

The title and the subtitle of this paper have been very deliberately chosen in order to express the boundaries within which I wish to confine my remarks.

First, I have chosen to speak of the doctrine rather than the dogma, and this calls for comment. The dogma itself is quite clear, even though it is often not accurately stated nor correctly understood; but when it is fully and accurately stated, as Pius IX intended it, then it is, I fear, an even greater stumbling-block in the path of Christian unity than is commonly believed. I shall begin therefore by stating the dogmatic or defined proposition of 1854, but the substance of this lecture is contained in the second half, where I deal with the doctrine, i.e. with the way in which one may understand and interpret the dogma.

Secondly, I have given the lecture a subtitle, 'Reflections on a Problem in Ecumenical Dialogue', to indicate the angle from which I want to speak about this doctrine. This paper consists simply of reflections, personal thoughts on the matter inspired largely by the many fruitful discussions I have had on the topic at meetings of this Society, and especially by the dialogue between Bishop Kallistos and Fr Yarnold, at our last meeting, in Chichester.

Thirdly, I want to reflect on it as a problem in ecumenical dialogue, and here again I should like to say something about the choice of words. I have deliberately not written the words 'as an ecumenical problem' because for most people it is not an ecumenical problem; in fact it never is, unless you get involved with the RCs. But I have deliberately chosen to speak of it as a problem in ecumenical dialogue because I think that this subject is a prime example, perhaps the best example in the world, of a topic where it is essential to know exactly what the words used mean. So often in discussing the doctrine of the Immaculate Conception, one finds people using the same words but understanding by them quite different things.

So let me end this introduction by reiterating the very limited aim of this paper: all I want to do is to try out on you some new ideas, new ways of looking at the dogma of the Immaculate Conception, in the hope that this may contribute to a clearer understanding in ecumenical dialogue.

1. *The dogmatic Definition of 1854*

It is hardly necessary to state that by the Immaculate Conception of the Blessed Virgin, the Roman Communion does not refer to a virginal conception, even though this is the meaning often attached to the words by people who hear the term 'Immaculate Conception' but have no acquaintance with Catholic theology. Yet even this crude misunderstanding can teach us something of value, for when we say that the Immaculate Conception of Mary does not involve her virginal conception, we have in fact stated that original sin (whatever meaning we attach to it) is not something which is essentially and necessarily transmitted by conception through sexual intercourse. This might be classed as a half-forgotten truth, for even the most conservative of theologians would readily admit that had our first parents produced children in the Garden of Eden, these children would not have been touched by original sin. Similarly, those who maintain that Jesus himself was the offspring of a union between Mary and Joseph must also confess that the so-called 'hereditary stain' of original sin is not passed on automatically through natural conception, as if it were something like a genetic characteristic, such as the colour of one's skin. I mention this now, because it will be of importance later.

What, then, does the definition of 1854 actually state? It is generally believed by well-informed Roman Catholics and others that Pope Pius IX defined 'that the most blessed Virgin Mary was, by a unique grace and privilege of almighty God, in view of the merits of Christ Jesus, the Saviour of the human race, preserved in the first instant of her conception from all taint of the original fault'. The words I have cited are, of course, a translation from the definition: but that is not the object of the definition. What Pius IX defined was, *that this doctrine is revealed by God.* That is why I said that when one has stated the dogma accurately, the problem becomes even sharper, for one must then ask 'Where is the evidence in Scripture, or even in apostolic tradition, for this assertion?'

I do not wish to talk about the reasons adduced to justify the definition, for that would require a paper of its own. But let me at least bring the problem caused by this definition into sharper focus by pointing to some factors which are not always taken into account by Roman Catholics when they seek to explain this dogma to others.

First, Roman Catholics, when they seek to explain this dogma to Christians of the Reformed Tradition, always - and rightly - point out that it does not assert that Mary was not redeemed, or that she did not stand in need of redemption. It is unequivocally stated in the definition that her preservation from the primordial taint was *both* by a quite singular grace and privilege of almighty God, *and* that it took place in view of the merits of Christ Jesus, the Saviour of the human race. All one need add is that the term 'privilege' is here used in its strict sense in legal Latin, where it refers to an exemption from a general law (*privilegium*, from *privatum* and *lex*). At this point, many Catholics think they have done their duty by their Reformed brethren, having explained to their own satisfaction how Mary was in fact redeemed.

Now it is true that they have in fact answered the first and most fundamental objection from the Reformed tradition, albeit principally to their own satisfaction. For one ought to observe that this is not in the specific sense an objection of the Reformers, in that it was not they who thought it up. It was in fact the standard objection of those medieval Latins who opposed the doctrine on theological grounds, more particularly in the Order of Preachers. Be that as it may, the Reformers adopted it, but did not adopt the medieval Latin answer from Duns Scotus, of preservative rather than liberative redemption. Catholics will nowadays stress, in dialogue with the Reformed tradition, that the argument of Duns Scotus, according to which Mary was by the grace of God preserved from ever being touched by original sin, means that Mary was even more wonderfully redeemed than we are; and that this redounds to the still greater glory of God, and of Jesus Christ, and of the Holy Spirit. And the same good Catholics often wonder why it is that highly intelligent Protestants cannot perceive this as a singular example of *Soli Deo Gloria*.

But the fact is that this is only part of the Protestant objection, and the part which is not of Protestant origin at all. More fundamental to the Protestant case is the deep and dearly-held conviction that all human beings, with the sole exception of Jesus Christ our Lord, are utterly and wholly corrupted by sin. Think of Luther, praying not that God would remove his sinfulness in this life, but that he would draw a veil over it; think of Calvin, and his views on the depravity of the human race. If Roman Catholics are going to engage in dialogue with their future fellow-citizens in heaven, then they have got to learn first to speak the language of Luther and Calvin, and they may find it is not so easy to translate their dogma into Lutheran or Calvinian. With Lutherans and Calvinists, the dogma of the Immaculate Conception poses a bigger problem than RCs think.

Let us turn secondly to Orthodoxy. For at least one hundred years every Roman Catholic seminary student has been taught that the Orthodox Church *de facto* accepts both the doctrine of the

Immaculate Conception of Mary and that of her bodily Assumption into heaven; that the earliest and most important witnesses to both doctrines are in the Christian East, in its liturgical feasts and in the homilies for these feasts; and that there is abundant and early evidence for the doctrine of the Immaculate Conception in the use of the terms such as 'immaculate, unstained, all-holy' by the Greek Fathers. For the young Roman Catholic seminarist preparing for an examination, it was an easy ride: Q.E.D.

And so it was, if one scanned the Orthodox horizon from the roof of St Peter's. Others could, of course, point out that there might be differences between the Greek and the Russian Orthodox tradition, which, if unimportant in Rome, were of importance in Orthodoxy, but I am not competent to discuss these; others may like to speak on this. One could also add that Orthodox bishops have, from time to time, had to warn the faithful that the mere fact that a dogma was newly defined by the Pope of Rome was not sufficient to make the doctrine heretical: thus, I believe, the Orthodox bishop in Paris informed his people that they need not cease to believe in the Assumption of the Blessed Virgin simply because Pope Pius XII had declared it a dogma of faith. But deeper, and very serious issues, are here at stake.

Paul VI was, as everyone knows, wholly dedicated to seeking reunion between Rome and the Orthodox Churches; and I would venture to say that no one in the entire world was more painfully conscious than he of the fact that the major stumbling-block lies in the Roman doctrines concerning the Papacy. It was to him a matter of agony. Now if we look at the two Marian definitions from the point of view of Orthodoxy, they exemplify to perfection the two major objections that the Orthodox Churches raise against Roman teaching about the Bishop of Rome.

(1) The Orthodox Churches would say that these two doctrines, however true, are *not* contained in Holy Scripture or in apostolic tradition, and therefore are *not* 'revealed truths'. Therefore both Pope Pius IX and Pope Pius XII were guilty of very grave error in proclaiming them to be such. Therefore the Pope of Rome is not, in the sense in which he claims to be, infallible.

(2) The Roman Church also claims that its bishop enjoys universal jurisdiction, a claim which implies that other local churches are in some way subject to the Bishop of Rome. Many Orthodox are deeply pained, and even offended, by the way in which the Roman See conducts its affairs with the Eastern Catholics: they see the Roman Congregation for the Eastern Churches frequently laying down the law on matters that have nothing to do with faith or morality, and doing so in a manner contrary to Eastern tradition. In short, the

Roman Church, for all its fine words, does not treat the Eastern Catholic Churches as sister churches, but simply as alternative liturgical rites in the Roman Communion; and the Congregation for the Eastern Churches is more like the Cabinet Office for Scotland or Wales than the residency for the High Commissioners of the Eastern Patriarchates. This is clean contrary to the whole Eastern tradition, and the Orthodox often feel that Rome habitually treats the Eastern Catholic Churches not so much as sister churches but as under-age daughters badly in need of parental guidance. The concept of one universal church has been pushed so far that it has rendered the complementary and necessary balancing concept of several local churches in practice obsolete. This is, I understand, the fundamental Orthodox objection to the doctrine of the universal jurisdiction of the Bishop of Rome.

For Orthodoxy, the supreme power in the Church is exercised *only* by an Ecumenical Council, and the Orthodox are unlikely to forget that they were not invited to Trent (which is therefore not an ecumenical Council but only a Western Synod), or to the First, or to the Second, Vatican Council (except, in the latter case, as observers, that is, on the same level as a number of Protestant laymen). Thus the papal definitions of 1854 and 1950, purporting to bind the Church universal, are but the ultimate proof of papal arrogance. Q.E.D. All that one might like to add is that the said definitions must be a godsend to Orthodox who want at all costs to preserve their Communion from reunion with Rome.

That is, I hope, a not unfair presentation of the scene. I know it is oversimplified, but that is how most Christians do in fact think. And the solutions proposed to the problems are often equally simplistic, because good Christians are so eager to see fulfilled the will of their Lord 'that all may be one'. Hence it is sometimes proposed, for example, that the Churches of the Reformation might not insist on the universality of sin, but would permit members of the Roman Communion to continue to believe in Mary's preservative redemption, if the Roman Church on its part would concede that this doctrine is not an essential article of the Christian faith. This would suffice as an implicit abandonment of the papal claim to infallibility and universal jurisdiction, in return for which the Bishop of Rome might be given some honorary but not executive primacy in a reunited Western Christendom. And similarly, if an Ecumenical Council could be summoned, the Orthodox Churches might very well be willing to negotiate a rephrasing of the two Marian dogmas, so that honour would be satisfied on both sides. Everyone knows, of course, that the Protestant plea to tone down the dogmas and the Orthodox insistence on the authority of an Ecumenical Council would in fact pull in opposite directions; but both views can be happily aired because everyone knows that the Roman Church is not going to budge anyway, and so the discussion is purely theoretical, and good Christians of all persuasions can sleep o'nights. I hope this is not an unfair picture of the *status quo*.

2. Reflections on the Doctrine

Where, then, do we go from here? During the discussion at Chichester between Bishop Kallistos and Fr Yarnold, one very fundamental difference between the Roman and the Orthodox approach was mooted, but was not, for lack of time, fully explored or argued out to an agreed conclusion, namely, the relevance of Mary's death for the dogma of the Immaculate Conception. It is on this point that I want to take up the discussion anew.

First, let us take the wording of the 1854 definition: 'preserved immune from all stain of original sin', or (if you prefer) 'preserved immune from all taint of primordial guilt'. In either translation we are faced with the concept of *labes culpae originalis.* In English, the usual terminology is that Mary was 'conceived without stain of original sin'. Let us accept that, and the next, inevitable question is, 'What is original sin, and in what does its stain, or taint, consist?'

Here one must turn to the Council of Trent, Session V, not merely because it is for Roman Catholics the most authoritative statement ever issued on original sin, but because it was this which Pius IX certainly had in mind when promulgating his Bull. Pius was saying that Mary was, from the first moment of her conception, untouched by original sin as defined by Trent.

So what does Trent say on the point? This was perhaps the thorniest problem the Fathers of Trent had to deal with, for they were far from agreed among themselves. In the end they did manage to produce an agreed dogmatic definition, but only by leaving several major problems unresolved (hence the origins of Jansenism etc.). Trent made one strong, anti-Lutheran assertion defining what original sin is not (see below, no. 4); but though it describes some effects of Adam's sin, it never came to any agreement as to what original sin as transmitted formally consists in, what it actually is.

So what did the Council of Trent in fact define?

(1) That Adam, as a result of his sin, lost holiness and righteousness; lost the friendship of God and incurred God's anger; lost the gift of immortality and was sentenced to die; passed under the power of the devil, and became in every way a less perfect creature. Thus canon 1, DS 1511=DB 788, a canon which reaffirms traditional teaching by combining two canons of Orange, nos. 1 and 19, DS 371 and 389 = DB 174 and 192.

(2) That Adam's sin affected his offspring as well as himself, and

that the damage consisted not merely in the transmission of bodily death as a penalty for sin, but in a truly sinful state which brought spiritual death to the soul. Thus canon 2, DS 1512=DB 789, also reproducing the Council of Orange, canon 2, this time almost verbatim (DS 372=DB 175).

(3) That 'original sin' in the descendants of Adam is something real, and not merely the imputation of Adam's guilt (canon 3, DS 1513=DB 790).

(4) That in the reborn 'original sin' is not to be identified with *concupiscentia*, i.e. that in those who are (by faith or baptism) justified, the inborn selfishness of the human race, and its propensity towards sin, are not of themselves sinful, but are only the result of our first parents' sin (canon 5, DS 1515=DB 792).

This is the description, then, of that which Pius IX says does not apply to Mary. So if we negative all the above statements, we should discover a description of what it means to say that Mary was from the first instant of her conception free from all trace of original sin. The list reads:

(1) she was from the first possessed of holiness and righteousness, was the object of God's love, endowed with immortality, and in no way under the power of Satan, as perfect a creature as Adam before the Fall;

(2) she was in no way destined to die, neither by bodily death nor by the spiritual death of the soul;

(3) she was different from all others in that she was in fact free from whatever is understood by original sin, whereas they are not;

(4) she is therefore free from all the inborn selfishness which is the lot of humankind, for that inborn selfishness and propensity towards evil are a result of our first parents' sin, and she was free from every trace of that sin.

Put it that way, and everyone sees at once the central problem, which Orthodox theologians have never ceased to stress. If Mary was in fact, according to the terms of Pius IX and the language of Trent, conceived without original sin, then she ought to have been immortal, should never have died (cf above, no 2). And though many Roman Catholics maintain that she did die, others have denied this, and in deference to the latter, Pius XII wrote in 1950, in the definition of the Assumption, only 'when the course of her earthly life was over', thus leaving the debate between Catholics open. Those who maintained that she did in fact die affirmed that, though she was by reason of her Immaculate Conception exempt from the destiny of mortality, it was eminently fitting that she should share in the passion, the redemptive passion, of her Son.

But when all that is said, the Orthodox objection remains in substance unanswered: if Mary was conceived immaculate, then, according to Trent, she was exempt from the destiny of death. But the Eastern Church, and especially the Orthodox Church, has for a millenium and a half celebrated the feast of her Dormition. She did die, and therefore the papal dogma of the Immaculate Conception is, in the terms in which it is stated, untrue; it is certainly not revealed by God, in Scripture or Holy Tradition; and it is certainly not what the Orthodox Church or the Fathers mean when they speak of the Theotokos as 'immaculate, unstained, all-holy'. The defining of Mary's Conception as Immaculate is therefore a most grave error, some would say a heresy, on the part of the Roman See, and the acceptance of this definition a lamentable fall from grace on the part of the entire Roman Communion. I hope that is a fair presentation of the case of those Orthodox who are most opposed to the Roman dogma. Is there any way forward?

I believe there is, and that a really thorough examination of this problem could be a paradigm for all ecumenical discussion or dialogue. For at this stage, it may seem that the whole paper has by now become a private conversation between Rome and Orthodoxy which is of little interest, perhaps even incomprehensible, to anyone from the Reformed tradition. But if we are sincerely searching for Christian truth, it is never sufficient to try to reconcile only two divergent traditions at the cost of ignoring others, and thereby alienating many other Christian communities. Our Saviour prayed that we may all be one, and it is too easy to forget that he said 'all', making no exceptions.

So at last to my personal reflections. First, it would be hard to find any educated person nowadays who, when not thinking about the story in Genesis of the Garden of Eden, believed that the first human beings were in fact immortal. And I take it that no one here believes that one thing can be true according to natural science, and the opposite true according to the faith. So let us assume that the first human beings were in fact mortal, and did in fact die.

Does this contradict the Bible, or the first canon of the Council of Trent, Session V? I think not, for we have to define very exactly what is meant by the term 'death', and I would suggest that it can be taken in two very different senses. The first is the normal sense, denoting the medical ending of earthly life, often painful; and I presume that this, the normal usage, is what is intended both by the author of Genesis and by the Fathers of Trent. In this sense, death is something to be feared, even dreaded, a penalty of sin, a result of sin, in that it overpowers every human being and seems to annihilate them.

But one can understand death in another sense, as denoting simply the coming to an end of life on this earth. This is the sense in which it is taken both in St John's Gospel ('he who believes in me, even though he should die, will continue to live, and everyone alive who believes in me shall never die', 11:25-26) and in the Roman Liturgy ('*vita mutatur, non tollitur*'). And, I am now going to be bold and add, in the Byzantine Liturgy and in the doctrine of the Orthodox Church. This latter fact is of immense importance for our present problem.

If one looks at the Byzantine Liturgy for the feast of the Dormition on August 15th, it is all about the transition of the Theotokos into life.

O wondrous paradox!
The spring of life is placed in a tomb,
and the grave becomes a ladder to heaven.

Everyone knows that, in Byzantine theology, the normal term to describe the end of Mary's life is the Dormition, her 'Falling asleep', though we encounter also the words 'Translation' (i.e. 'Transfer') and 'Passing over'. Her Dormition is also described as 'All-holy', 'Most sacred' and 'deathless'; by it, she is 'translated from life to life' (Great Vespers, Tone Five).

But two texts from Mattins seem to me of especial importance, because one of them contains the only mention of Mary's 'death' that I have found in the liturgy, and the other one serves to refine it, and to define it further. I cite them in the version given by Bishop Kallistos and Mother Mary in their edition of *The Festal Menaion* (pp 516-7).

Thy death, O pure Virgin, was a crossing into a better and eternal life. It translated thee, O undefiled, from this mortal life to that which knows no end and is indeed divine; and so thou dost look in joy upon thy Son and Lord. (Canticle IV, First Canon).
O pure Virgin, sprung from mortal loins, thine end was conformable to nature; but because thou hast borne the true Life, thou hast departed to dwell with the divine Life Himself.' (Canticle III, Second Canon).

Two points may here be noted: (1) that Mary's death is 'a crossing into a better and eternal life', and (2) that 'her end was conformable to nature'. Others infinitely more versed than I in Byzantine Liturgy will, I hope, take up this point, and correct me if I am wrong, but I think that one has to be very circumspect in speaking about the death of the Virgin, and that, on the rare occasions where it is mentioned in the Byzantine liturgy, it is always immediately qualified.

So what I am suggesting is this: that Mary did in fact truly die, in the ordinary, medical sense of the term, with heart failure, or a thrombosis, or of some other cause, so that there could in fact have been a perfectly normal death certificate. But I am also saying that for her, because of her Immaculate Conception, that is, because of her holiness and righteousness, this medical death was not in any sense the dreaded visitant envisaged by the author of Genesis or the Council of Trent. Her departure from this world is not in any way to be compared with the scene in Part I of Newman's *Dream of Gerontius*, or with the cacophony of the chorus of demons in Part II.

Indeed, I know of no more inspired description of the Blessed Virgin's departure - dormition - death - assumption - what shall we call it? - than the lines of Francis Thompson:

Thy Son went up the angels' ways,
His passion ended; but, ah me !
Thou found'st the road of further days
A longer way to Calvary.

On the hard cross of hopes deferred
Thou hung'st in living agony,
Until the mortal dreaded word,
Which chills our mirth, spake mirth to thee.

The Angel Death, from this cold tomb
Of life, did roll the stone away,
And he thou barest in the womb
Caught thee at last into the day.

Now that seems to me something which all Christians, whether of the Reformed or of the Catholic or of the Orthodox tradition could reasonably accept.

I suggest that this is by human criteria quite a reasonable view to hold. I suggest that it harmonises perfectly with the Roman Catholic dogmas of the Immaculate Conception and of Mary's Assumption, body and soul – i.e. as a person – into heaven, and that these dogmas are therefore not contrary to human reason. I would respectfully submit that there is no intrinsic reason why an Orthodox Christian should not assent to the assertions made in those definitions about the Blessed Virgin, even though they may not be able in conscience to accept that these are truths revealed by God.

None of this, of course, proves that these definitions are true, or that it was wise or prudent of the Popes to define these doctrines, much less that it was necessary to define them. But even the most dedicated anti-papalist would willingly confess that they concentrate the mind with startling clarity on some very central issues of the Christian faith, and I am not speaking of the papal claim to doctrinal infallibility which by Roman Catholic standards is not in fact, when correctly understood, a *central* doctrine of the faith at all. When I say that these two Marian definitions serve to concentrate attention on some central doctrines of the faith, I am thinking of the doctrines of grace and redemption, of the boundless generosity of God's giving, of his transformation of our sinful race, through the merits of his Son, into a people wholly and entirely redeemed, in body and soul. The two Marian definitions have placed these other topics concerning grace and redemption firmly at the forefront of ecumenical discussion, at which all Christians, I trust, can rejoice. But once the dialogue starts, it is not sufficient that the participants should listen to each other with total charity; they must also be quite sure of what each person means, assumes or implies, by every word or concept brought into the discussion.

The feast of Mary's silence: the entry into the Temple (21 Nov)

Rt Rev Kallistos of Diokleia, M.A., DPhil.
Orthodox, Pembroke College, Oxford

If I were a doctor and were asked for my advice,
I should reply: Create silence!
Søren Kierkegaard

Many of you will have read the remarkable novel *Silence* by the Japanese writer Shusaku Endo, in which he speaks about the silence of God; and doubtless you will also know Joseph Pieper's work *The Silence of St Thomas*. I have often wondered whether anyone has written a book called *The Silence of Mary*. Recently to my delight I learnt that there is indeed a book with precisely such a title;[1] but since it is in Spanish and as yet untranslated, I have not so far read it. Mary's silence is surely a subject that deserves to be explored. For silence is not simply negative, an absence of sound, a pause between words. Silence is positive and creative, one of the deep sources of our being, a primary, objective reality, which cannot be traced back to anything else or replaced by anything else. 'Silence', it has been said, 'belongs to the basic structure of man';[2] without the dimension of silence we are not genuinely human. The Blessed Virgin Mary, then, as pattern and model of what it means to be a person – after Christ her Son, the mirror in which we see reflected our own true human face – must surely exemplify this essential human quality of silence.

There is, I believe, a day in the Church's year which can be seen as the celebration of Mary's silence: the feast kept on 21 November, known in the East as the Entry of the Mother of God into the Temple, and in the West as the Presentation of the Blessed Virgin Mary. This is admittedly one of the less well-known of the Marian festivals. Although reckoned in the East as one of the twelve great feasts of the Byzantine liturgical year, it is in practice somewhat neglected, enjoying far less prominence in Orthodox popular devotion than 25 March or 15 August, or even than the Nativity of the Mother of God on 8 September, all three of which are likewise reckoned among the twelve major feasts. In the Latin rites of the West it has never been more than a minor feast.

The feast first emerged in the East, and while its origins are obscure it is undoubtedly ancient. It seems to be linked especially with the basilica of St Mary the New in Jerusalem, dedicated on 21

November 543, and possibly it began as the annual dedication festival of this particular church. By the second half of the seventh century it had come to be celebrated generally throughout Jerusalem, and by the early eighth century the festival was also being kept in Constantinople.[3] Its appearance in the West is much later, dating only from the late fourteenth century. A French nobleman familiar with Greek worship, Philip of Mezières, while the representative of the King of Cyprus at the Papal court, persuaded Pope Gregory XI to introduce the feast at Avignon, where it was celebrated for the first time on 21 November 1372. Even though in the Latin rites it has remained a lesser observance, in certain circles it has been kept with particular honour: in the Company of St Sulpice, for example, it is the custom to renew the promises of tonsure on 21 November, while the Order of the Company of Mary Our Lady, founded in Bordeaux by St Jeanne de l'Estonnac in 1607, holds a procession through the gardens in its schools on that day, ending with a special act of consecration by the girls to the Virgin Mary. Somewhat surprisingly, the feast was even marked by a public holiday in late nineteenth-century Prussia.[4]

For the present-day worshipper, whether Western or Eastern, the Feast of the Entry suffers the disadvantage of lacking any foundation in Scripture, entirely based as it is on an apocryphal source, the *Protevangelion* or *Book of James*.[5] This Greek work, dating from the middle of the second century – probably known to Justin Martyr and to Clement of Alexandria, and certainly to Origen – has had a profound influence on Marian devotion and liturgical practice. The *Protevangelion*, which is also the basis for the liturgical texts used in the Byzantine rite on 8 September, begins by describing the grief of the elderly couple Joachim and Ann, who had been disappointed in their hopes of offspring. In her prayers Ann promised God that, if granted a child, whether male or female, she would dedicate it as a gift to the Lord. To her joy, soon afterwards she conceived and bore the Virgin Mary. When the child reached the age of three, Ann felt that the time had come to carry out her promise, and so she and Joachim decided to take Mary to dwell in the temple. But Joachim did not want the young child to be parted in sorrow from her parents, and so he gathered together the young girls of the neighbourhood to form an escort, carrying lamps and lighted torches in front of Mary. The plan was successful. Captivated by the torches, she joyfully followed the other children into the temple, not once looking back at her parents or weeping as she went to dwell in her new home. Zacharias the high priest welcomed her at the entrance to the sanctuary, making her sit 'upon the third step of the altar'. She dwelt day and night in the Holy of Holies, fed miraculously by the hand of an angel. When she reached the age of twelve, the priests felt that it was no longer fitting for her to remain in the holy place, and so Zacharias betrothed her to Joseph.

What are we to make of this story? It may well have a certain historical basis. Elizabeth, the wife of Zacharias, was related to the family of the Virgin Mary; and so this Jewish priest – incidentally in Luke's narrative he is nowhere described as high priest – may perhaps have played a part in her early upbringing. Admittedly this is no more than a speculation. But there can certainly be no historical basis whatever for the belief that Mary lived for nine years in the Holy of Holies. Indeed, the legendary character of the story has long been acknowledged, and for this very reason Pope Pius V (1566-72) deleted the feast from the Roman calendar, although it was reinstated by Pope Sixtus V in 1585. Grave doubts about the historicity of the *Protevangelion* were also expressed by Byzantine scholars, although the church hierarchy reacted sharply to this. The historian Nicephorus Gregoras (1295-1356/60) was actually excommunicated for asserting that the Virgin could not possibly have entered the Holy of Holies.[6]

Literal, historical fact is not, however, the only form of truth. May there not be another level of truth, symbolic yet none the less real, hidden within the story of Mary's childhood years in the temple? For a possible answer it is natural to look first at the hymnography for the feast in the Byzantine service books.[7] *Lex orandi lex credendi*: our faith is expressed in our prayer. Christianity is a liturgical religion. Worship comes first, dogmas and discipline second. How, then, is the entry of the Mother of God into the temple understood in the liturgical texts? We should not expect to find a simple answer, for with its complex layers of meaning Byzantine worship resembles the *Anathemata* of David Jones. At least five themes recur constantly in the office for the feast:

(1) First and most obviously, Mary is seen as being herself the true temple. The real sanctuary is not the building of wood and stone but the 'living temple' that is the person of the Holy Virgin.[8] 'She is indeed the heavenly tabernacle', states the *Kontakion* in its refrain, while in the hymns she is described as 'ark', 'holy of holies', 'house of God' and 'house of grace'.[9] The dwelling-place of God incarnate is not a shrine constructed by human hands, but the altar of Mary's body and soul.

(2) Developing the temple *motif* in a different way, the hymnography speaks of the Virgin at her entry into the sanctuary as a sacrificial offering dedicated to God: she is 'an offering without blemish', 'a three-year-old victim of sacrifice'. She is also likened to the incense-offering: 'as acceptable incense she is offered in the holy

temple ... she is offered to the Lord in the temple of the Law as a sweet-smelling fragrance'.[10]

(3) On this as on so many other feasts, the liturgical texts explore the symbolism of light. The Mother of God is compared to a lamp burning in the temple: 'the three-lamped light' of the Trinity 'makes you burn, O Theotokos, in the temple of his glory'; she is a 'candlestick with many lights'.[11] Mary, as the 'lamp that bears the divine light', is several times contrasted with the lamps and lighted torches carried by the children in procession: 'The young girls rejoice today, and with lamps in hand they go before the spiritual lamp and lead her into the Holy of Holies... You have appeared in the sanctuary accompanied by brightly-burning lamps, who are yourself the receiver of the divine light that no one can approach.' [12]

(4) A more far-reaching theme present in the liturgical texts is that of predestination and preparation. Mary's unique vocation, so it is emphasized, did not commence only at the Annunciation, but she is 'the Mother preordained before all ages', 'the preordained Queen of all', 'forechosen from all generations to be the dwelling-place of Christ'.[13] She was marked out and preselected by God before the creation of the world, and the whole history of the Old Covenant points forward to her. This is a truth underlined equally in the liturgical texts for 8 September, the feast of Mary's Nativity.[14] Forechosen in this way from eternity, she was the special object of God's providential care from the moment of her entry into the world. From her earliest childhood God prepared her for her preordained task, and her time of seclusion within the temple forms part of this preparation. As Ann her mother says to her in one of the *aposticha* at Vespers, 'Go into the place which none may enter: learn its mysteries, and *prepare youself* to become the pleasing and beautiful dwelling of Jesus.'[15]

(5) Permeating all the hymnography of the day and giving to the feast a distinctive flavour, there is an ever-present note of rejoicing. For Orthodoxy the Mother of God is *par excellence* a sign and expression of joy. In the Liturgy of St Basil she is termed 'the joy of all creation', while the *Akathistos Hymn* invokes her as 'joy of all generations', and in her icons she is designated by such titles as 'Joy of all who sorrow' and 'Unexpected Joy'. This same sense of the joy of Mary permeates the observance of 21 November. The texts of the day repeatedly refer to the joy of Joachim and Ann, the joy of Zacharias, the joy of the young girls in the festal procession, the joy of the Holy of Holies, but they speak above all about the joy of the Virgin herself. Here the hymnography takes up the beautiful words in the *Protevangelion*: 'The priest received her and kissed her and blessed her.... And the Lord put grace upon her and she danced with her

feet and all the house of Israel loved her.'[16] Mary, state the hymns for the feast, 'dances for joy as she goes round the divine habitations', 'partaking of boundless joy in the temple'.[17] And the joy which Mary experiences she also shares with us: she is 'the joy of all', 'the cause of our joy', 'mediator of joy for the world'.[18] As she enters the sanctuary, the angels cry aloud: 'Joy and deliverance is led into the temple.'[19]

What the liturgical texts do not mention, at any rate in an explicit way, is the silence of the Mother of God. This forms, however, the master-theme in what is possibly the greatest of all the sermons composed for this feast, the homily of St Gregory Palamas (1296-1359) *On the Entry into the Holy of Holies and the Godlike Life within it of our Most Holy Lady the Ever-Virgin Mary*.[20] According to Palamas's biographer, Patriarch Philotheos Kokkinos, this was one of the earliest of the saint's writings, composed around the year 1334 while he was living on Mount Athos, before he had become involved in the controversy with Barlaam the Calabrian about the divine light of Tabor and the uncreated energies of God. Kokkinos adds that Palamas was moved to write the homily because certain persons, not named, 'with rash and ignorant tongue dared to insult those mysteries';[21] this is possibly a reference to the sceptical Gregoras.[22] But in fact Palamas makes no attempt in the homily to prove the historicity of the events celebrated on 21 November. Instead he treats Mary's entry into the temple as a symbol of the mystical ascent of the soul to God, interpreting the story somewhat as St Gregory of Nyssa interprets the ascent of Sinai in his *Life of Moses*. This seems to have been an original idea of Palamas's own, and I have found no examples of such a treatment in the earlier homilies on the feast that I have examined.[23]

Earlier we thought of Mary's years in the temple as a time of preparation, in which she was made ready for her future task as Godbearer. But what, we may ask, was the particular form taken by this preparation? She was prepared, answers Palamas, by acquiring that inner depth which is conferred by silence. Palamas sees her as a contemplative, as the supreme hesychast, the one who more than any other has attained true *hesychia*, stillness or silence of heart. Entering the temple, she severed all links with secular and earthly things, renouncing the world, living for God alone,[24] choosing a hidden existence invisible to outside eyes, a 'life of stillness'.[25] Enclosed within the Holy of Holies, her life was like that of the hermits and ascetics who dwell in 'mountains and deserts and caves of the earth' (cf Heb. 11:38).[26] Her period in the temple was thus a 'desert' experience, an anticipation of monasticism. There she learnt to subject her 'ruling intellect (*nous*)' to God,[27] leading an angelic life,[28] attaining *theoria* or contemplation,[29] and practising continual prayer.[30] Transfigured by the divine light, she saw the uncreated God reflected in the purity of her heart as in a mirror.[31] And her means of access to all these mysteries of inner prayer was precisely *hesychia*, stillness:

> It was holy stillness that guided her on her path; the stillness which signifies cessation of the intellect and of the world, forgetfulness of things below, initiation into things above, the shedding and transcending of thoughts. Such stillness is true action, the ascent to genuine contemplation or, to speak more truly, to the vision of God.... She alone among all humankind from such an early age practised stillness to a surpassing degree.... She made a new and secret road to heaven, the road – if I may so express it – of noetic silence.[32]

Some of you may feel that this eloquent portrayal of Mary the hesychast, the model of contemplative union, bears little relation to the village girl of Nazareth described by St Luke. Yet is there not in fact a connection? *Hesychia*, stillness or silence of heart, is basically nothing else than an attitude of attentive listening. In the words of Max Picard, 'Listening is only possible when there is silence in man: listening and silence belong together.'[33] 'Be still and know that I am God' (Ps. 46:10): the Psalmist's phrase sums up the essence of silence. To be silent in prayer is to listen to God. 'Silence is a presence', says Georges Bernanos; 'at the heart of it is God.' Silence, so understood, is not emptiness but fullness, not the absence of speech but the awareness of God's immediacy. Silence is waiting on God. Now in the gospels Mary is depicted precisely as *the one who listens*: who listened to the word of God at the Annunciation (Luke 1:38; cf 11:28), who 'kept all these sayings, pondering them in her heart' (Luke 2: 19; cf 2:51), who told the servants at the marriage feast in Cana to listen to her Son (John 2:5). The Mary of Palamas, Mary the hesychast in the temple, turns out in the end to be not so very different from the Mary of St Luke's Gospel who listens to God in humble and attentive silence.

Such, then, in part, is the symbolic meaning of the feast of the Entry of the Mother of God into the Temple. It speaks to us of joy: Christianity, so it reminds us, came into the world as 'glad tidings of great joy' (Luke 1:19, 2:10), and if we do not feel this 'great joy' in ourselves we are not truly Christian. Yet more profoundly, it speaks to us of creative silence. 'Understand through the stillness', said Dag Hammarskjöld; 'act out of the stillness; conquer in the stillness.' That exactly is the lesson to be learnt from this present feast.

'Man is what he does with his silence.' Von Hügel's *dictum* can best be interpreted in the light of a statement by G.K. Chesterton:

'Men are men, but Man is a woman.' Mary is our human ikon and paradigm. Through what she did with her silence – that silence set before us symbolically in the story of her years in the temple – she is an example and an inspiration for us all.

Notes

1. Ignacio Larrañaga, *El Silencio de Maria* (Buenos Aires 1977)
2. Max Picard, *The World of Silence* (London, no date), 15.
3. See H. Leclercq, in *Dictionnaire d'Archéologie Chrétienne et de Liturgie* XIV (Paris 1948), cols. 1729-31; E. Mercenier and G. Bainbridge, *La prière des Eglises de rite byzantin* II, l (2nd ed, Chevetogne 1953), 142; I.E. Anastasiou, in *Thriskevtiki kai Ithiki Enkyklopaideia* V (Athens 1964), cols. 451-4.
4. K.A.H. Kellner, *Heortology: A History of the Christian Festivals from the Origin to the Present Day* (London 1908), 266; O. Caudron, in *Dictionnaire de Spiritualité* XII (1984), col. 1311.
5. Greek text in C. Tischendorf, *Evangelia Apocrypha* (2nd ed, Leipzig 1876), 1-50; Eng trans in M. R. James, *The Apocryphal New Testament* (Oxford 1924), 39-49. The account of Mary's entry into the temple is in §§vii-viii. cf, Hilda Graef, *Mary: A History of Doctrine and Devotion* I (London 1963), 35-7.
6. F. Miklosich and I. Müller, *Acta et Diplomata Graeca Medii Aevi* I (Vienna 1860), 490: act of excommunication by Metropolitan Philotheos of Silyvria (undated).
7. See *The Festal Menaion*, translated by Mother Mary and Archimandrite Kallistos Ware (London 1969), 164-98. In the quotations that follow, I have sometimes modified the translation.
8. *The Festal Menaion*, 174.
9. Ibid, 185, 166, 192, 184.
10. Ibid, 169, 170, 194, 192.
11. Ibid, 165, 182. Cf Exod 25:31f.
12. Ibid, 167, 173.
13. Ibid, 170, 172.
14. See *The Festal Menaion*, Introduction, 48.
15. *The Festal Menaion*, 171.
16. *Protevangelion*, §vii, 2 (trans M. R. James, 42).
17. *The Festal Menaion*, 171, 184.
18. Ibid, 181, 183, 172.
19. Ibid, 186.
20. *Homily* 53: ed P.K. Christou, *Ellines Pateres tis Ekklisias* 79: (Thessalonica 1986), 260-347. *Homily* 52 (238-57), written apparently at a later date, in the 1350s when Palamas was Archbishop of Thessalonica, is also devoted to the feast of the Entry, but says noth-

ing about the silence of the Mother of God.

21. *Encomium on the Life of Gregory Palamas*, iv, 38 (Migne, *PG* [*Patrologia Graeca*] 151, 581C; ed P. K. Christou, *Ellines Pateres tis Ekklisias* 70 (Thessalonica 1984), 148. But Christou (*Ellines Pateres tis Ekklisias* 79, p.14) thinks that in its present form *Homily* 53 dates probably from 1341.

22. J. Meyendorff, *Introduction à l'étude de Grégoire Palamas* (Paris 1959), 391.

23. I have looked at the two homilies on the Entry by St Germanus, Patriarch of Constantinople (d. c. 733) (*PG* 98, 291-320); the homily by St Tarasius, Patriarch of Constantinople (d.806) (*PG* 98, 1481-1500); the three homilies by George of Nicomedia (late ninth century) (*PG* 100, 1401-56); and the homilies by Leo VI the Wise (886-912) (*PG* 107, 12-21), Theophylact of Bulgaria (d.c. 1126) (*PG* 126, 129-44), Iakovos Kokkinovaphos (*PG* 127, 600-32), and Isidore of Thessalonica (1342-96) (*PG* 139, 40-72). None of these treats Mary as the model of the hesychastic life or emphasizes her silence within the temple, although Isidore speaks of her continual communion with God (§22 [64B]).

24. *Hom*, 53, §47 (ed Christou, 322); §50 (324, 326).

25. §21 (286, 288).

26. §22 (288).

27. §18 (282).

28. §45 (318).

29. §49 (324).

30. §59 (338).

31. §53 (328).

32. §§52 (328), 53 (330), 59 (338).

33. *The World of Silence*, 177.

The power of chastity for Mary and her sisters: the empowerment of women in the poetry of Prudentius

Professor Rebecca Weaver
Presbyterian, Union Theological Seminary, Virginia

My choice of Prudentius may, on the face of it, appear somewhat dubious. A Spaniard with a distinguished career in the civil service,[1] Aurelius Prudentius Clemens subsequently earned an honoured place in Christian literature for the poetry and hymns which he composed. Yet although he wrote extensively about Christian faith and practice, he left no work specifically concerned with the Virgin Mary. The references which he did make to Mary are fairly brief. She is never the central figure in a scene, never the subject of intense scrutiny.

The role of the Virgin was for Prudentius simply not a matter of controversy: her position in the drama of human salvation required no defence and little clarification. Yet it is his very ease in speaking of the Virgin that I find significant. For the unfettered freedom with which he made assumptions and drew conclusions suggests that his views regarding Mary and her relationship to other Christians, specifically Christian women, were hardly peculiar to him. Thus by considering passages from Prudentius we may be able to get a glimpse of the unquestioned images of Mary and of Christian women which pervaded the religious circles that Prudentius inhabited.

Prudentius's life spanned the decades of the early ascendancy of Christianity. He was born in AD 348, only thirty-five years after Constantine and Licinius had granted toleration to Christianity[2] and thereby introduced an era of almost unimpeded expansion for the church. When Prudentius himself was about thirty-two years old (380), the Emperors Theodosius and Gratian made Nicene Christianity the official religion of the empire, outlawing all opposition, both pagan and heretical. Although the date of Prudentius's death is uncertain, he seems to have died just prior to the sack of Rome (410) by Alaric. In other words, Prudentius lived at a peculiar time in history. His writing career encompassed that brief period when it was possible to be boundlessly optimistic about the possibilities for social and personal transformation within a unified Roman Empire officially subject to the lordship of Jesus Christ.

This transformation of human life through Christian faith and practice is a central concern of Prudentius's work, and it is with regard to this preoccupation that the role of the Virgin Mary and of her kinswomen emerges. My procedure in considering his writings will be, first, to examine instances in which Prudentius referred to the Virgin Mary in order to ascertain his understanding of Mary's contribution to the transformation of human life brought about through Christ. Second, I will isolate instances in which Prudentius has portrayed the transformation of particular women and see what, if any, relation these women bear to Mary.

Cathemerinon

One collection of hymns composed by Prudentius was entitled *Cathemerinon* (*The Daily Round*). Each of these hymns was written for use either at a particular time of the day or at a specific season of the Christian year. The references to Mary in this collection occur not only in predictable contexts, such as in 'A Hymn for the 25th of December' and in 'A Hymn for Epiphany,' but also in somewhat unexpected settings, such as 'A Hymn Before Meat.'

As the title suggests, 'A Hymn Before Meat' offers praise to God for the bounty of the earth, particularly for the gifts of the table. But amidst the praise is an admonishment to Christ's followers that these divine gifts do not give licence for abuse. One must be on guard that eating does not serve as an occasion for sin, as in fact it had in the case of Adam and Eve. For at the instigation of the serpent, Eve had induced Adam to partake of the forbidden fruit, and through this unholy meal our first parents had sinned, thereby forfeiting the integrity of the human condition. In consequence, the woman, until now a virgin, was subjected to the man; the serpent's head was put under the woman's foot;[3] and the rebellion begun by our primeval ancestors came to be perpetuated in each new generation.

This reference to the predicament brought about through the virgin Eve allowed Prudentius to introduce, in a parallel familiar to the early church, the remedy made possible through the Virgin Mary.[4] A new scion has arisen, a second man, the Word of God whose virgin mother crushes the serpent with her foot.

> The Word of the Father becomes living flesh pregnant by the shining Godhead, not by wedlock nor espousal nor allurement of marriage, a maid inviolate bears it. This was the meaning of that age-long hate, that quarrel to the death between snake and man, that now the serpent on his belly is crushed by a woman's feet. The virgin who proved worthy to give birth to God subdues all its [the snake's] poisons, and the snake, its length twisted in coils it cannot unravel, feebly spews its harmless venom on the green grass whose hue it matches. (3.141-155)[5]

Two characteristics of this passage are significant for our study. First, although in the larger framework of the hymn it is clearly to Christ rather than to his mother that Prudentius has addressed his prayer and worship, it is not nearly so clear who actually achieves the radical victory over the serpent. At the very least it must be said that although Christ may have introduced a new untainted race, it is his mother who overcomes the power of the serpent. [6]

Second, it is Mary's worthiness which allows her to give birth to the enfleshed God and thus the new race, and that worthiness is also presumably the source of her power for the subjugation of the serpent. Significantly, the only hint that Prudentius provides as to the source of Mary's worthiness is her virginity. [7]

Thus in a hymn otherwise intended to invoke Christ's blessing on prudent eating, we find two striking Marian themes almost inadvertently introduced: first, the awesome, although somewhat ambiguous, role of Mary in subduing the power of sin and thereby altering the human condition and, second, her virginity as the apparent source of her power. Prudentius's casualness in introducing the themes suggests that for him these points required no defence. As we shall discover, the occasional, but consistently undefended, re-emergence of these themes throughout his writing, further suggests that these notions surrounding Mary were so well established, at least in the poet's mind, that they were not subject to question.

In fact, Prudentius appears so convinced of the inherent power of Mary's virginity that he does not limit its beneficial effects to Mary alone. Her son also profits from his mother's purity. In 'A Hymn for Epiphany' Prudentius examines in grisly detail the slaughter of the young male children at the command of Herod.

> Amid so many deaths Christ alone is reared unharmed. While the blood of His generation flowed, the virgin's child alone has escaped untouched the sword that robbed young married mothers of their babes. (12.137-140)

At least one clue to the invulnerability of the infant Christ seems to lie in the chastity of his mother. Certainly his is an invulnerability which the children of married mothers lack. In this account of the slaughter of the Holy Innocents we get a glimpse of the empowerment of Christ through the purity of his mother. Mary's purity and the benefits which her son, and finally we, derive from that purity are at the very heart of Prudentius's understanding of the Virgin.

In a final hymn from the *Cathemerinon*, 'A Hymn for the 25th of December,' the importance of the virtue of chastity in defining Mary is made explicit. The poet addresses the yet unborn Christ:

> Come forth, sweet boy. Thy mother is chastity herself, a mother yet unwedded. (11.13-16)

Prudentius has here depersonalized Mary by a simple identification of her with the virtue of chastity. Admittedly, several lines later he restores to Mary the peculiarly personal, motherly elements which one might expect in this hymn celebrating Christmas Day. But even as he addresses the new mother, he makes clear that the glory which is to come to her throughout the ages will be directed not so much to her as to her purity.

Feelest thou, noble maiden, through thy weariness now come to its time, that the undefiled glory of thy purity waxes with the honour of the child thou bearest? (11.53-56)

It is as chastity itself that Mary will be remembered and exercise her power, at least in the poetry of Prudentius.

In these sparse but striking references to Mary in these hymns from *The Daily Round* what we find is a somewhat depersonalized figure characterized almost exclusively by her chastity. For it is because of her chastity that she overcomes the serpent, that her son is secured against the sword of Herod, and that finally she is venerated.

Apotheosis

We will find somewhat different emphases in the *Apotheosis* (*The Divinity of Christ*) a hymn of nearly 1,100 lines written to defend the faith against a variety of opponents both within and without the church. As in the *Cathemerinon* the references to the Virgin are somewhat limited.

In one of these references, as Prudentius defends the church against its pagan detractors, he speaks of the collapse of pagan religion and dates that collapse from the moment of the virginal conception.

Since the Spirit, that Spirit who is God, touched a mortal womb and God entered into a mother's body and by a virgin made himself man, the cavern of Delphi has fallen silent, its oracles condemned....No longer does a priest possessed utter with foaming mouth and panting breath fates drawn from Sibylline Books....Ammon returns no answer in the deserts of Libya. The very Capitol at Rome laments that Christ is the God who sheds light for her emperors and her temples have fallen in ruins at her leaders' command. (436-446)

Prudentius has conflated a slow, centuries-long process of Christianisation of the Empire into a single moment. It was at the virginal conception itself that the idols were vanquished and oracles rendered dumb. It is by God's action in Mary that the religion of the Empire has been rendered ineffectual.

Of course, Mary is hardly the prime actor. In fact, again addressing the pagans, Prudentius speaks of the Word made flesh as a temple to which Mary had made a negative contribution.

This is the temple thou [pagans] hast attacked, seeking to take it with scourge and cross and gall. It was cast down in destruction by tormenting pains. Be it so, for from the mother's womb it had what could be destroyed: but that which, of the mother's part, was undone in brief death, the third day restores to life by the majesty of the Father. Thou hast seen my temple, by whose protection I am saved, rise on high with companies of angels. (527-533)

Prudentius leaves no doubt that the flesh taken from the Virgin is an indispensable component of that temple by which salvation comes. Nevertheless, Mary's contribution stood in need of improvement. It was subject to suffering and death; it had to be restored to life by the divine majesty. But once restored, it was exalted to the heavens, made everlasting, inseparably joined to the source and guarantee of our salvation.

Thus, in arguing against the pagans Prudentius has introduced a new, negative dimension in his portrayal of Mary, i.e. the frailty of the humanity which the Word takes from her. Nevertheless, he gives far greater attention to the positive outcome of the divine-human union: in this transaction of debased nature and deity, human reality has been immeasurably transformed for the better. Mary's gift of frail nature has become an essential element in the exaltation of humanity.

This dual aspect of Mary's role becomes clearer later in the *Apotheosis* in Prudentius's attack against fellow Christians who taught the divinity of the soul. According to Prudentius the soul prior to baptism is caked with the sins of its ancestors. Following baptism the soul still remains liable to sin, for it is joined in communion with the flesh. Each provokes the other to sin, and together both soul and flesh suffer the torments of punishment. But

From these torments Christ sets us free, for He alone had a mother immaculate and wore a sinless body; Jesus put on a nature liable to punishment, but not a nature liable to the contagion of sin, and so He owed no debt to punishment, being undefiled, without sin, free from all besmirching fault. (932-937)

Prudentius seems to be suggesting here that Christ's ability to save us from punishment is to be attributed, not to his deity, but to the immaculate character of his mother and to the sinless body which he received from her. It was a body undefiled, not liable to the contagion of sin. Prudentius's earlier statements in the hymn regarding the frailty of the flesh which God the Word received from Mary can now be understood in a somewhat qualified sense. The frailty appears to pertain strictly to human liability to punishment, animal liability to death, but not to any liability to sin.

Mary's chastity functions as a safeguard against any propensity to sin. Her purity ensures that her son's human nature is immune to sin.[8] Moreover, his sinless body, taken from his chaste mother and owing no debt to punishment, frees us from sin as well. The benefits of Mary's virginity are far-reaching, to say the least. Her chastity provides her son with an immunity to sin, ensures that he owes no debt to sin, and, at the same time, frees us from sin.

Somewhat less extreme and certainly more familiar claims regarding Mary can be found elsewhere in the *Apotheosis* as Prudentius argues against the Ebionites. Ebionites are generally identified as Jewish Christians from the first centuries who acknowledged Jesus as the Messiah but denied his deity. Predictably, against such opponents, Prudentius emphasized the circumstances of Christ's conception and birth.

> We believe that He springs from no earthly seed, takes no unclean beginning from sin-stained man. It is the subtle fire that begets Him, not a father's flesh nor blood nor foul passion. The divine power weds a maid inviolate, breathing its pure breath over her untainted flesh. The strange mystery of his birth bids us believe that the Christ thus conceived is God. The unwedded maid is wedded to the Spirit and feels no taint of passion. The seal of her virginity remains unbroken; pregnant within, she is untouched without, blossoming from a pure fertility, a mother now, but still a maiden, a mother that has not known husband. (564-575)

In this passage what the poet calls our attention to is not so much the miracle that Mary should have conceived without male intervention but that the conception was utterly untouched, uncontaminated by passion; she was left fully intact. Her chastity of spirit as well as of body was never violated. The proof of Christ's deity lies not so much in the absence of a human father but in the absolute chastity of his conception. But chastity alone was not enough. Faith was necessary, as well. At the visitation of the angel,

> The holy virgin herself believed that shining minister's prophecy, and therefore because of her faith she conceived Christ. For Christ comes to those who believe; the doubting heart, whose faith falters, He rejects and will not honour. Her maidenhood and ready faith drink in Christ in her womb and lay Him up in the pure secrecy of her heart, to bring Him forth in due time. (579-584)

Unlike the heretical Ebionite, Mary believes the message of the angel. And her faith joined with her chastity are the means for her reception of the Word. Accordingly, she is a model not only for the heretic but also for the Christian, for anyone who seeks God.

Prudentius is careful, however, to isolate faith, apart from chastity, as the necessary prerequisite for our own reception of Christ. The desirability, if not necessity of virginity, is, nevertheless, clearly implied.

In these scattered citations which we have noted in the *Apotheosis*, it has become increasingly clear that the virginity of Mary functions as a far-reaching explanatory device for the possibility of the incarnation, the sinlessness of Christ, and the transformation of the human condition. These extraordinary effects of her virginity would seem to distance not only Mary herself but also her remarkable purity from anything even remotely resembling ordinary Christian experience. Yet as we have just heard, the Virgin functions for Prudentius not only as a critical contributor to the divine work of salvation but also as a model for its appropriate reception. In later hymns this awesome power of chastity will come to be seen as accessible to others as well.

Psychomachia

Before examining specific instances of remarkable Christian achievement, specifically the achievements of chaste women, we need first to consider in more general terms the process of transformation by which the soul is empowered to these attainments. Prudentius has described that process in glorious and gory detail in a long allegorical poem, the *Psychomachia* (*The Fight for Mansoul*).

The poem is a vivid depiction of the prolonged warfare between the virtues and the vices for possession of the Christian soul. Both sets of qualities are anthropomorphized as female. In a long series of bloody forays, Faith conquers Worship-of-the-Gods, Chastity vanquishes Lust, Long-Suffering overcomes Wrath (actually Long-Suffering assists in all the battles), Lowliness subdues Pride with the inadvertent assistance of Deceit and the determined cooperation of Hope; Soberness preserves all the virtues against Indulgence; Greed disguised as Thrift is undermined by Good Works. And finally Concord rallies the other virtues to prevail against Discord, who is also known as Heresy. With the major vices and a host of minor ones at last conquered, Faith, the queen of the virtues, ensures that the newly purified soul is suitably adorned as a temple in which Wisdom (Christ) reigns supreme.

It should be noted here that although the warfare between the flesh and the spirit, the vices and the virtues, is a continuous internal struggle in the heart of each person who would follow Christ, the struggle is not entirely an individual matter. Particularly with regard to the combat between Chastity and Lust, it becomes clear that victories by our predecessors in the faith in their struggles against Lust have, to some degree, weakened the dread hold of Lust on those of us who come after.

Thus Prudentius cites the bloody death of the lustful Holofernes at the hand of the chaste Judith (Jdt 13) as having diminished the power of Lust in the world as a whole. And Judith, by her triumph, prefigures Mary in whom Lust is, in fact, overcome. The new state of affairs for all humankind is made clear in the exultant victory speech by Chastity over Lust.

Since a virgin immaculate has borne a child, hast thou [Lust] any claim remaining – since a virgin bore a child, since the day when a man's body lost its primeval nature, and power from on high created a new flesh, and a woman unwedded conceived the God Christ, who is man in virtue of his mortal mother but God along with the Father? From that day all flesh is divine, since it conceives Him and takes on the nature of God by a covenant of partnership....neither has God lessened what is his by taking on what is ours, but by giving his nature to ours He has lifted us to the height of his heavenly gifts. It is his gift that thou liest conquered, filthy Lust, and canst not, since Mary, violate my authority....No more, thou chief of fiends, tempt thou the worshippers of Christ; let their cleansed bodies be kept pure for their own king.' So spake Chastity, and rejoicing in the death of Lust, whom she had slain, washed her stained sword in the waters of Jordan. (70-100)

In the battlefield of the Christian soul, chastity has conquered Lust, but it is clearly God the Word who, through the incarnation, has made that victory possible. His virgin mother functions as the pivotal figure in whose flesh that victory is first accomplished and by whose flesh that victory is communicated to us. In the virginal conception of Christ the human condition has been radically altered in two ways: Lust has lost its claim upon us, and all flesh has been made divine.

First, Lust loses its claim by the fact that the human nature of Christ was conceived without it. An immaculate virgin gave birth to a son. The necessity of passion was severed. Of course, Prudentius does not suggest here that the biological requirements for conception have been removed in the case of anyone else, but he does seem to be indicating that sexual passion is no longer an inevitable, governing force of life.[9] Even if it cannot be entirely removed, since Mary it has lost its authoritative claim upon us.

The second way in which the human condition has been transformed is that all flesh has been made divine. In Mary's immaculate body, human flesh conceived Christ. The enormous power of what Prudentius is saying here is best captured in a quotation taken from another of his hymns, the *Hamartigenia* (*The Origin of Sin*). Here Prudentius is praising Ruth the faithful daughter-in-law of Naomi.

Ruth...proved herself worthy of the hand of Boaz, and being taken in pure wedlock she conceived and gave birth to the family of Christ, David's royal line, and numbered God along with her mortal descendants. (785-788)

The relationship between God and humanity has changed dramatically if God is to be numbered among the descendants of Ruth. The relationship has been changed into a kind of unequal partnership in which each member takes on properties of the other. God assumes frail human nature, and human nature is made divine. This dramatic change occurs not only for Ruth, who because of her purity became an ancestress of Christ, but for the rest of us as well by means of the flesh which we share with Christ through Mary.

In Prudentius's references to the Virgin Mary two characteristics have emerged: the nearly exclusive identification of Mary with the virtue of chastity and the extraordinary transformation which has taken place in human nature through the divine employment of that chastity. What we must do now is look at the evidence of that transformation which Prudentius found in the lives of actual Christians. It is my intent to limit my investigation to cases of women. I do so partly for practical reasons of economy but also because of the eminent, if numerically limited, position which chaste Christian women hold in the poetry of Prudentius.

As we have already discovered, Prudentius depicts human nature prior to the incarnation, i.e., the nature taken from Mary, as frail. It is debased animal nature, and in some hymns he is explicit about the character of that frailty. For example, in 'The Hymn Before Meat', which we noted earlier, Prudentius details the losses which were incurred through the fall.

Then the treacherous serpent beguiled the simple heart of the maid to seduce her male partner and make him eat of the forbidden fruit, being herself doomed to ruin in like manner. Each other's body (unlawful knowledge), after eating, they saw uncovered, and their sinful lapse brought the blush to their cheeks: covering they made by stitching leaves, that modesty might veil their shame. Trembling before God for the guilt they felt, they were driven out from the abode of innocence, and the woman, till then unwedded, came under a husband's rule and was commanded to submit to stern laws. The wicked serpent, too, that devised the guile, was condemned to have its three-tongued head bruised by the woman's heel; so the serpent was under the woman's foot, as the woman under the man. Following their lead, succeeding generations are corrupted and rush into sin, and through copying their primitive ancestors, lumping right and wrong together, pay with death for their rebellious deeds. (3.111-135)

Several points are striking. First, Prudentius speaks of the woman prior to the fall as unmarried, a simple virgin. With sin came carnal knowledge, attendant shame and guilt, loss of innocence, marriage, and death. And marriage, for the woman, at least, consists of submission to bitter conditions. Immediately, we see that the unwedded life, for the woman anyway, recaptures to some extent the innocence of Eden. This view of marriage, of course, was hardly peculiar to Prudentius. What is important for our purposes is its relation to the Virgin Mary, who unwedded, becomes the bearer of a Second Man, a new race, which lacks the faults of the offspring of Adam.

By the explicit contrast which he sets up between Eve and Mary and their respective progeny, Prudentius makes clear that as Christians are members of this new race they are not merely the heirs of Christ but also the offspring of the Virgin Mother, Mary, Chastity herself.[10] In contrast to the daughters of Eve, a Christian woman should emulate her mother Mary through an unwedded life.[11] To marry would not only forever exclude her from Eden but would also place her in a difficult subjection to a husband. Moreover, the chances are enormous that she would be burdened with children just as ill behaved and ungovernable as those of Eve. In the eyes of Prudentius the virgin life offered a woman at least a partial reprieve from the penalties exacted for original sin.

His intention, however, was not to suggest how the burdensome conditions of women's lives might be alleviated. Instead, what he did was to call attention to the chasm which separates those women who have chosen to follow Christ, particularly virgins, from their non-Christian counterparts. His somewhat random comments about women in general suggest that Prudentius, on the whole, had a rather low opinion of the capacities of females, but his extravagantly laudatory descriptions of female Christians point to the miraculous transformation which God can accomplish on despicable human frailty.

For example, in the *Hamartigenia* Prudentius described with evident distaste the use of adornment by women.

> It were wearisome to detail all the profane trouble matrons take, who colour the forms which God has dowered with his gifts, so that the painted skin loses its character and cannot be recognised under the false hue. Such are the doings of the feebler sex, in whose narrow mind a frail intelligence tosses lightly on a tide of sin. (273-278)[12]

Prudentius did acknowledge that men are guilty of indulgence as well. The point here, however, is that the poet clearly had a fairly low estimation of women as a group. He found expressions of feminine vanity to be repugnant. Yet that view is in stark contrast to his profound admiration for chaste Christian women, for elsewhere he extols consecrated virgins and those widows who have remained celibate.

> These are the Church's necklace, the jewels with which she decks herself; thus dowered she is pleasing to Christ. (*Pe* 2. 305-307)

The image is startling.[13] It is through the attractive purity of its chaste women that the Church is made pleasing to Christ. The power of chastity, especially the chastity of women, has now become critical to the union of the Church with Christ. [14]

Prudentius does make clear, however, that virginity alone, apart from commitment to Christ, lacks this transformative power. He draws a sharp contrast between the thoroughgoing purity of Christian virgins and that of their pagan counterparts, the Vestal Virgins.[15] Just being a virgin is not enough. It is a matter of being a Christian virgin that brings about the transformation of a woman.

Peristephanon

The most dramatic examples of this transformation are found in the *Peristephanon* (*The Crowns of Martyrdom*), a collection of fourteen poems[16] celebrating the victories of early Christian martyrs. Despite the numerical preponderance of heroic Christian men in these hymns, the females whom Prudentius did portray emerge as awesome figures. We will consider three of them.

The martyr Eulalia, a girl of twelve, undoubtedly embodies the poet's ideal for the behaviour of a young Christian girl. Scorning toys, jewellery, and prospects for marriage, she 'practised the manner of hoary age.' (3.25) The persecution of Christians in a nearby town aroused Eulalia to disobey her mother and flee the safety of her secluded country home in order to join the ranks of the martyrs. In her journey through the dark countryside at night Eulalia is accompanied by angels and guided by the same light which had guided Israel through the wilderness. Clearly the message is that God will protect and bring to fruition such single-minded devotion. And, in fact, the next morning the barely adolescent Eulalia presents herself to the Roman authorities whom she boldly berates for ungodliness.

> With the heart in her young breast panting for God, female as she was she challenged the weapons of men. (3. 34-36)

The Roman governor, although obviously angered, attempts to dissuade her with reason. He implores her to consider what she is losing.

> Think of the great joys you are cutting off, which the honourable

state of marriage offers you. The family you are bereaving follows you with tears, your noble stock mourns over you in distress, because you are dying in the bloom of youth when you are just reaching the age of dowry and wedlock. Does not a rich and splendid marriage appeal to you, nor the love of your elders, which you ought to respect, whereas your rash conduct is breaking their hearts? (3. 104-113)

In response Eulalia spits in the governor's face and kicks over the images of the gods. Immediately she is tortured and burned, her soul wings its way to heaven as a dove, and now generations later she serves as a patroness in heaven for the town of Emerita where her ashes are interred and she is revered.

She, set at the feet of God, views all our doings, our song wins her favour, and she cherishes her people. (3. 213-215)

The hymn suggests several convictions of Prudentius regarding female Christians. First, commitment to the unmarried life by a young girl is seen as good. To turn to God seems to be equated, at least in the case of Eulalia, with renouncing the marriage bed. Second, desire for God replaces feminine weakness with awesome courage, if not arrogance. The young girl rushes out to challenge, even scorn, the Roman government. Third, marriage and submission to parents are presented, not as Christian values, but as Roman values. Love for God would appear to set a young woman on a plane far above these lesser, earthly attachments. Undoubtedly for Prudentius devotion to God, demonstrated in chastity, separates a Christian female, young or old, from the weaknesses inherent in her gender and empowers her to overcome all earthly authority and values. Having renounced her sexuality, in Christ she becomes truly a new person on earth as well as a formidable figure in heaven.

Eulalia's connection to Mary is not explicit, but clearly this chaste soul is a daughter of Chastity herself. Her courage in the single-minded pursuit of God is indicative of the character of the new race born of Mary.

As an aside, it may be noted that the description of the martyrdom of Eulalia is rich with classical allusions, particularly phrases drawn from Virgil's *Aeneid*. In one parallel, Prudentius speaks of Eulalia in terms which Virgil had employed in connection with Ascanius, the son of Aeneas. In the *Aeneid* the young Ascanius serves as a symbol for Rome's future glory. By the use of a literary parallel, Prudentius has now given that exalted position to Eulalia: Rome's real glory lies not in the illustrious descendants of Aeneas but in a new race, the fearless Christian martyrs symbolized in the young Eulalia. Moreover, the courage that Prudentius attributes to the girl far exceeds anything which Virgil grants to the boy.[17] Even though she is only a female, the Christian virgin would appear to possess a strength of character far exceeding the capacities of pagan male.

But, of course, all Christian women did not remain unmarried or suffer martyrdom. In the account of a mother who must watch the torture and decapitation of her young son, Prudentius provides a picture of exemplary Christian fortitude.

Although it was the boy who was, in fact, executed, the intent of the Roman official was to punish the mother by forcing her to witness the suffering of her son. Her crime had been to teach her son of Christ, the Holy Spirit having taught her, apparently without intermediary. The vindictiveness of the Roman official is wasted on this mother, however. She, strengthened by her fidelity to Christ, simply does not respond as an ordinary mother would.

As Prudentius describes the scene, the crowd, even those administering the torture, weep as the boy's body becomes bloody from the lashes. It is only the mother's eyes that remain dry. And when the child, in thirst, cries for water, she rebukes him.

> I suppose, my son, you are upset by a weak fear and the dread of the pain casts you down and overcomes you. This is not what I promised God the child of my body would be, this is not the hope of glory for which I bore you, that you should be able to retreat before death! (10. 721-725)

She urges him to emulate the obedience of other martyred sons, the Holy Innocents and the Maccabean brothers, and even Isaac, who had been willing to serve as a sacrifice for his father. In this appeal to the child, the mother is invoking a tradition in which parents, particularly mothers, have given up their sons for God.

The ultimate paradigm of maternal obedience and loss was, of course, the Virgin Mary. Although Prudentius never makes the comparison explicit, details in the scene surely suggest it. The lack of any reference to a father, the fidelity and fortitude of the mother, the innocence of the son, the stripes inflicted on him by the soldiers, reference to his death as a cup from which he must drink, and the power accruing to the son through that death·all intensify the impression that this mother and son are re-enacting, on a lesser scale to be sure, the roles of Christ and Mary. This impression is strengthened when, at the moment of his death, she entreats him:

> Farewell, my sweetest, and when in blessedness you enter Christ's kingdom, remember your mother, changing from son to patron. (10.833-835)

And as her son's neck is severed from his body, she sings a hymn:

> Precious is the death of a holy one in the sight of God; he is thy

servant, the son of thine handmaid. (10. 839-840) [18]

The mother has remained with her son to the end, never flinching, never resisting the sacrifice made to God.

Although we are dealing here with a small boy and a dominant mother, the similarities to Prudentius's own presentation of Christ and his mother could hardly be unintentional. This handmaiden of the Lord, through her single-minded fidelity, has empowered her son to win the victor's crown. And in his victory she wins a protector in heaven. The Christian mother has assumed attributes of the Virgin Mother.

The transferral of the powers of Mary to others is made even more explicit in the case of Agnes, a young Christian about thirteen years old who was martyred for her faith in Rome.[19] During her trial she angers the Roman judge by her fearlessness when threatened by torture and death. Shrewdly recognizing that chastity is dearer to Agnes than life, the judge has ordered her to be placed nude in an area where prostitutes are solicited. But Agnes remains unafraid. She insists that

He [Christ] stands by the chaste and does not suffer the gift of holy purity to be defiled. (14. 34-35)

And in fact, the crowd honours her modesty and looks away. The one unlucky fellow who dares to stare at her is immediately struck blind and almost dies. But according to Prudentius, by some accounts the virgin Agnes intercedes to Christ and the man's sight and health are restored. Christ not only protects the virgin from defilement but also hears her prayers on behalf of others.

Martyrdom, however, still lies ahead, and Agnes embraces it joyously.

Now the disembodied spirit springs forth and leaps in freedom into the air, and angels are round her as she passes along the shining path. (14. 90-92)

Agnes looks down upon the earth with all its frailty, inconstancy, and vanity.

All this Agnes tramples on and treads under foot as she stands and with her heel bears down on the head of the fierce serpent which bespatters all earthly things in the world with his venom and plunges them in hell; but now that he is subdued by a virgin's foot he lowers the crests on his fiery head and in defeat dares not to lift it up. Meanwhile with two crowns God encircles the un-wedded martyr's brow. (14. 112-120)

The enraptured poet concludes his poem with a prayer to the virgin martyr.

O happy virgin, glory unknown before, noble dweller in the height of heaven, on our gathered impurities turn thy face with thy twin diadems, thou to whom alone the Father of all has granted the power to make a very brothel pure! I shall be cleansed by the brightness of thy gracious face if thou wilt fill my heart. Nothing is impure which thou dost deign to visit in love or to touch with thy restoring foot. (14. 124-133)

Through her virginity and fidelity Agnes has attained something of the stature of Mary. Whereas in the 'Hymn Before Meat' it was the virgin mother of Christ who had bruised the serpent's head and thereby lessened the power of sin, here it is the virgin martyr who is credited with having that power.

Agnes not only personally profits from the double crown of virginity and martyrdom, but in turn she bestows benefits on us. That she works for our purification (and thus salvation) through her own purity recalls the power and benefits of Mary.

In conclusion I would point out that feminist studies are increasingly calling to our attention the power, both religious and social, which frequently accrued to women in the early church who chose the celibate life.[20] Our reading of Prudentius suggests that he had little, if any, interest in the social aspects of this empowerment. On the other hand, a more enthusiastic witness to the religious aspects of this empowerment would be difficult to find. Prudentius appears convinced that fidelity to God, expressed in virginity, or to a lesser extent in faithful motherhood, effects a transformation in female nature such that woman is indeed a new creature, a daughter or kinswoman of Mary, a key figure in the accomplishment of human salvation.

For Prudentius the image of the female Christian has been shaped by his portrait of Mary. The daughters of Mary not only partake of the divinization of human life accomplished through God in the Virgin, but these daughters also partake of the attributes of Mary in their own chaste victory over sin.

Notes

1. Prudentius, *Praef* 16-21. Bernard M. Peebles, *The Poet Prudentius* (New York: McMullen Books, 1951), 13-15, 17-18. Anne-Marie Palmer, Prudentius on the Martyrs (Oxford: Clarendon Press, 1989), 24-31.

2. Edict of Milan, 313

3. For a discussion of the history of interpretation of Gen 3.15, see Hilda Graef, *Mary: A History of Doctrine and Devotion* (London: Sheed and Ward, 1985), 1-3.

4. See Hans von Campenhausen, *The Virgin Birth in the Theology*

of the Ancient Church, trans Frank Clark (Naperville, IL: A.R.Allenson, 1964), 41. Campenhausenn notes that the first attempt to place Eve and Mary in parallel with reference to the serpent occurs in Justin *Dial* 100. 4f. See also Thomas Boslooper, *The Virgin Birth*, (Philadelphia, Westminster Press, 1962), 31.

5. All quotations of Prudentius's poetry are from *Prudentius*, 2 vols, trans H.J. Thomson, Loeb Classical Library (Cambridge, MA: Harvard University Press, 1969, 1979).

6. cf Irenaeus, *Haer.* 3.22.4 and Ambrose, *Inst virg* 13.81.

7. Prudentius does not seem to suggest that the worthiness or purity of Mary derives from the Word within her.

8. See Campenhausen, 76-79, for the connection first made by Ambrose between the virgin birth of Christ and his sinlessness.

9. See Elaine Pagels, *Adam, Eve, and the Serpent*, 73-74, 96, for a discussion of conviction of early Christians that they possessed moral freedom, especially power over the passions.

10. cf Ambrose, *Inst virg* 94.

11. Graef, 53. In the fourth century, at least among ascetics in Egypt, the 'imitation of Mary' was by now an established way of life.'

12. cf Juvenal, *Satires* 6.457.

13. cf Ambrose, *Exp. in Ps* 118.17.18.

14. Campenhausen, 45-46, cites a variety of instances in the writings from the early church in which women who contribute to the salvation of God's people are portrayed as types of the new Eve. His point is that the Eve-Mary typology was not originally limited to a Mariological interpretation. There were many Marys.

15. 'Our virgins too have their noble rewards – modesty, the face covered with the holy veil, honour in private while their figure is unknown to the public, feasts seldom and slight, a spirit ever temperate, a law of chastity that is discharged only with death. Hence fruit an hundredfold is brought into their barns, barns never exposed to a thief in the night, for no thief assails heaven, and the seal of heavenly things is never broken by dishonesty; it is on the earth below that dishonesty is planned.' (*Contra Symmachum* 2. 1055-1063)

16. Palmer, 86-97.

17. Palmer, 159f. cf Virgil, *Aeneid* 1.646; 4.274-276.

18. I am suggesting that for Prudentius the *ancilla* of Ps 115 (116) 15-16 is the *ancilla* of Lk 1.38.

19. cf Ambrose, *Hymnus* 65; Damasus, *Epigram* 40, Ihm.

20. Elizabeth A. Clark, 'Ascetic Renunciation and Feminine Advancement: A Paradox of Late Ancient Christianity,' *Ascetic Piety and Women's Faith* (Lewiston, New York: Edwin Mellen Press, 1986), 175-208. Pagels, 87-89.

Mary In Eastern Church literature

Archimandrite Ephrem Lash
Orthodox, Monastery of the Assumption, Yorks

1. Introduction – the Question of Typology

Some months ago, when Dom Alberic proposed this title to me, I accepted because it seemed sufficiently vast, or vague, to enable me to talk about pretty well anything I liked; but when I came to assemble the notes I had been making, to try to arrange them in some sort of order, I realised that the title was in fact 'The Mother of God in the Old Testament'. This is because at the heart of the Eastern Churches' contemplation of the Mother of God and her role in the economy of salvation lies their firm belief that the two Testaments form a single revelation, and that the whole of the Old Testament looks forward to, typifies, or, one could say, is an icon of the New. If one of the keys to the understanding of Christian spirituality is St Paul's injunction to 'pray without ceasing', one of the keys to the understanding of Christian hermeneutics is his assertion that 'every scripture is inspired and useful for teaching'; or, as the Vulgate and the Peshitta understand it, 'every inspired scripture is useful for teaching'. [2 Tim. 3:16][1] For present purposes the difference between these translations need not concern us. There is an important hermeneutical principle involved here, one which the Church inherited from the Synagogue: everything in the Bible is there for a purpose. If, for example, Genesis 14 gives us the exact number of Abram's servants, then God must have a reason for it, and it is the task of the Christian, or Jewish, exegete to search out that reason. Modern Christians have a tendency to find all those genealogies in Chronicles, or all the ritual details in Leviticus boring, and irrelevant to their living the Christian life. This is no new problem, as we can see from the following remark of St John Chrysostom:

> I haven't prolonged my talk without purpose, but because there are some uncouth people who, whenever they take the Holy Bible in their hands and find either a list of dates or a catalogue of names, skip over them at once and say to anyone who rebukes them: 'but it's just names; nothing useful!' What's that? God is speaking and you, you dare to say there's nothing useful in what is said?[2]

This sort of remark can be paralleled in many other passages from St John, and he, it is well to remember, is on the whole thoroughly Antiochene in his exegesis. More recently, forty years ago to be precise, in a paper on the Mother of God to the Fellowship of St Alban and St Sergius, Fr L.S. Thornton re-echoed St John's words: 'nothing in the Old Testament can safely be ignored by the Christian theologian'.[3]

Until the rise of what is known as the 'critical', or sometimes the 'scientific', study of the Bible such an understanding of Holy Scripture was normal. As the late Professor Lampe, in an important paper entitled *The Reasonableness of Typology*, wrote: 'until this development took place, the unity of the Bible was the fundamental premise on which all were agreed. A common belief linked the authors of the New Testament books with their readers. This was the conviction which they shared; that the whole Bible spoke directly of Christ, in prophecy, type and allegory so far as the Old Testament is concerned...'.[4] One might argue, on the basis of Luke 24:27 and 44, that it was the view of the incarnate Lord as well. It is also a basic presupposition of nearly all traditional expressions of Christian piety. How many couples choose as one of the hymns for their weddings that Christian targum on Psalm 22, 'The King of Love my shepherd is'? The only alternative seems to be some form of Marcionism, with the assertion, not infrequently heard from ostensibly Christian pulpits, that the God of the New Testament, unlike the God of the Old, is a God of love.

If the Old Testament in its entirety is to maintain its place in our churches today as part of the revealed word of God, then I submit that typology is one of the principal means by which it will be so maintained. At about the time that Geoffrey Lampe wrote his paper on typology, the Bishop of Oxford sent a letter to his clergy reminding them that the lectionary was not simply an anthology of the incumbent's favourite passages of Scripture. St John Chrysostom would have agreed. Lampe writes: 'There would seem to very many Christians to be sound reason, and not merely pious fancy, in the liturgical reading of the history of the Exodus and the Passover at Eastertide.' He continues, 'the problem before us is to discover some means of distinguishing between helpful and misleading forms of typology; we have to try to separate those which can be rationally explained and defended from those which are far-fetched.'[5] Some years later Professor Dennis Nineham, whom none could suspect of being a dyed in the wool traditionalist, made a similar observation in his Cadbury lectures. For the Churches of the East, at least, one criterion for a legitimate type is its consecration in the tradition of the *lex orandi*.

To say that is also, I believe, to say that such a reading of Scripture is not part of the public and missionary proclamation of the Gospel. The use of Old Testament types as part of Christian apologetic, as proof texts to demonstrate the truth of Christian doctrines, is seldom successful, as St Justin had already discovered in the second century. Rather it is part of the inner heart of the Church's meditation on God's word. The Church, like Mary, keeps or watches over certain things in her heart, and among them is the mystery of Mary herself. The Russian theologian Vladimir Lossky wrote, 'it is hard to speak and not less hard to think about the mysteries which the Church keeps in the hidden depths of her inner consciousness. Here every uttered word can seem crude; every attempt at formulation can seem sacrilegious. The Mother of God was never a theme of the public preaching of the Apostles; while Christ was preached on the housetops, and proclaimed for all to know in an initiatory teaching addressed to the whole world, the mystery of his Mother was revealed only to those who were within the Church'.[6] The poets and preachers, the teachers and the hymn-writers who spoke and sang of Mary had only two 'doctrines' as the foundation of their contemplation: that she is Ever-virgin and that she is Mother of God incarnate. Most, if not all, of them knew very large parts of the Scriptures by heart, and in their meditation on the word of God they found images, icons, of the mysteries of Mary, Mother of God and Ever-virgin, on nearly every page of the Old Testament, from Genesis to Daniel. I do not, moreover, believe, as many modern critics of typology suppose, that they sat down consciously to 'find' types; rather, as day by day they contemplated God's word, heard it proclaimed, sang it in psalms and canticles, these types and images would have sprung spontaneously to their minds. Their theology emerges from prayer and contemplation, from *lectio divina* in its old sense; it is not the product of what the Fathers, particularly St Ephrem, call 'prying' or 'inquisitive investigation'.

It is clearly not possible for me to attempt an exhaustive survey in the time available, and if my choice of texts appears somewhat random, that is because I have had to make do with what I have around me in my own small library; though this is not perhaps such a disadvantage as it may appear, since one of the most striking things about the whole Eastern tradition is the extraordinary consistency of the imagery. For every text I have chosen, whether in Greek, Syriac, Coptic or Ge'ez, I could have chosen a dozen others which employ the same images. From the second century for more than seven hundred years the liturgical tradition of the Eastern Churches, even though divided by the tragic schism that followed Chalcedon in 451, is, in this respect at least, unbroken and undivided.

2. Mary and Eve

St Paul saw in Adam a type of Christ, the second Adam, and from here it was an easy step to see in Eve a type of Mary, and this may well have been the first Old Testament type to have been applied to her by the Church. Certainly it was current in the second century and we find it both in St Justin and in St Irenaeus. As with St Paul's use of the First and Second Adam typology, so with Mary and Eve, it is a typology by contrast: Eve's disobedience is reversed by Mary's obedience; in the words of St Irenaeus:

> And as by means of a virgin who did not obey, humanity was smitten, fell and died, so by the Virgin who hearkened to the word of God, humanity, once more revived, by life recovered life.[7]

St Romanos, in the sixth century, also stresses, in a number of places, the contrast between the two virgins, Eve and Mary. Here is a stanza from his second Kontakion on the Annunciation, which was used on the 26th of December, the day of the Mother of God in the Byzantine calendar. The Archangel Gabriel is speaking:

> Adam was thrust out: and therefore Adam's God,
> arranging for Adam's rising,
> Took him from your womb:
> Of old a woman cast him down,   and now a woman raises him
> again,   a virgin from a virgin.
> Then Adam   had not known Eve,
> Nor Joseph now   the Mother of God,
> But without seed
> A virgin bears a child,   and after child-birth
> remains still a virgin. [8]

St Irenaeus in the passage from his *Demonstration of the Apostolic Preaching*, from which I quoted just now, also contrasts the birth of the First Adam from the virgin earth with that of the Second Adam from the Virgin Mary:

> But whence was the being of the first-formed man? From the will and wisdom of God and from the virgin earth. 'Because God had not sent rain upon the earth, says the Scripture, before humanity was created and man had not tilled the earth.' But God took up some of the dust of the earth when it was yet virgin and created man as the beginning of humanity. But the Lord, wishing to restore man again, accepted the economy of the Incarnation, and was born of the Virgin by the will and wisdom of God, that He might shew that He had a body like Adam's, and that He was, as it was written in the beginning, 'man according to the image and likeness of God'. [9]

St Ephrem, in the fourth century, in his *Commentary on the Diatessaron*, develops this further:

> Mary gave birth without the participation of a man. Eve was born from Adam without there having been any carnal union, so it is with Joseph and Mary, the Virgin, his spouse. Eve brought the

murderer Cain into the world: Mary the Giver of Life. Eve brought into the world the one who shed his brother's blood: Mary Him whose blood was shed by his brothers. Eve saw the one who trembled and was a fugitive on the earth because of the curse: Mary Him who assumed the curse and nailed it to the tree of the Cross.

By the virginal conception learn that He who brought Adam into the world without carnal intercourse from the virgin earth, also formed the Second Adam without carnal intercourse in the Virgin's womb. And because the first Adam had gone back to his mother's womb, by the Second Adam, who did not go back to the womb, he who was buried in his mother's womb was brought back.[10]

In his first *Hymn for the Nativity* St Ephrem again draws the parallels between Eve and Mary, and it is perhaps worth noting that he makes Adam, not Eve, responsible for the fact that women have to endure the pains of labour:

Adam brought pains on the woman who had come forth from him:

Today, she who gave birth to the Saviour has repaid the pains.

To Eve the giver of birth a male gave birth, who himself had no birth:

How much more should Eve's daughter be believed, who without a male has given birth to a child.

The virgin earth had given birth to Adam, ruler of earth:

The Virgin today has given birth to Adam, ruler of heaven. [11]

This contrast between the virgin earth and the Virgin Mary is, I believe, one of the main sources for the image of Mary as the 'untilled field', which occurs constantly in the hymns of the Byzantine tradition, though St Proclus also compares Mary to the 'Field which the Lord has blessed' from Isaac's blessing of Esau (Gen.27.27). [12]

In the Semitic languages, as in Greek and Latin, 'obeying' is 'hearing', and so we find the contrast developed by the Fathers between the poison which the serpent breathed into Eve's ears and the Medicine of Life, to use a favourite Syriac title for Christ, who entered Mary's ears at Gabriel's greeting. A hymn for the feast of the Annunciation in the Syrian church puts it like this:

The serpent with his twisted plots
Breathed poison in the careless woman's ear;
The poison spread to every generation and slew the nations,
Until from Mary was born
This Child, who slew the monster.
The Word of the Father came down

Towards the ear, entrance of evil,
Followed the serpent's example and noted his tracks;
By his coming down he expelled
The poison from the pure one's ear.

Just as the poison, that destructive beguilement
Of the serpent, had entered by the ear,
That by the gate of death life might enter,
And that, instead of sin,
The goodness that reigns might be made manifest,

The Father sent Gabriel,
Faithful Messenger of the Word,
To bring to the Virgin the peace which brings joy,
And that the war might be ended and destroyed
Which the Evil one had sown in Eden. [13]

Both Mar Ephrem and Mar Jacob of Sarugh say that if women wear pearls in their ears it is really in honour of the Incarnation. Here is Mar Jacob in a long, poetic digression in a letter to the monks of the monastery of Mar Bass:

If I am hung from the ear,
    It is to crown the hearing of women,
Who were worthy to receive by their ears
    The Word, the Pearl
Which the Father gave to save the world,
    Like the veil on which is depicted the image of the light,
I am hung from the ears of young women
    To honour the ear which served as gateway to the Word.
When He was pleased to dwell in a young woman,
    I was placed as guardian of the gate,
Outside the gateway of the ear
    To honour the abode in which He dwelt. [14]

The ancients believed that the pearl was produced by a flash of lightning penetrating the ocean depths and, as it were, impregnating the oyster. It was therefore a perfect image of the Incarnation. In a Canon for Sunday in Tone One we read:

Let us hymn her who without seed and above nature bore Christ, the pearl of great price from the divine lightning. [15]

In both Greek and Syriac the particles of consecrated Bread of the Eucharist are frequently referred to as 'Pearls'. St Ephrem begins his series of hymns *On The Pearl* by taking a pearl in his hand and examining it from every side, and, as he says, it becomes a spring from which he drinks the mysteries of the Son.

Again it is Mary,

That I saw there
And her pure conceiving;
The Church too
And the Son in her womb
Like the cloud
Which carries Him;
Type of heaven
From which beams
His radiant splendour. [16]

The 'cloud' is an allusion to Isaias 19.1: 'Behold, the Lord rides on a light cloud and enters Egypt. And the idols of Egypt will be moved at his presence; and the heart of Egypt will melt in the midst of him'; a verse traditionally understood as an allusion to the Flight into Egypt, and the 'light cloud' as an image of the Mother of God.

Unlike most precious stones, which need cutting and polishing, the pearl is beautiful by nature; it is naked and unadorned, like Eve in Paradise, who was naked, yet clothed in a robe of light:

You are like Eve
Who was clothed
Although she was naked.
Cursed be the one who deceived her,
Stripped her, abandoned her!
But the serpent could not
Strip you of your glory.
By the mysteries of which you are the sign
Women have been clothed
With Light in Eden. [17]

The last lines of this passage from the third hymn on the Pearl are a reference to Baptism. The disobedience of Eve had shut the gates of Paradise, it is Mary's obedience which opens them to all mankind, who enter them by Baptism into the death of Christ on the tree of the Cross. St Irenaeus, after contrasting the disobedience of Eve with the obedience of Mary, continues:

the transgression, which had come about by means of the tree was abolished by the Tree of obedience. [18]

This tree is of course the Tree of the Cross, but it is also the Tree of Life, which is in the midst of Paradise, whose fruit is Christ. The poet Theophanes in his Canon for the feast of St Leo of Rome writes:

Unharmed by the tree of knowledge, I pluck ripe life; for you, Immaculate, the Tree of Life, burgeoned Christ, who makes known to all the entrances to life; therefore, All-pure, we faithful magnify you as Mother of God. [19]

The same idea is found in a series of twenty hymns to the Mother of God attributed to St Ephrem, but which are probably somewhat later:

> Mary gave a sweet fruit to mankind,
> And, instead of that bitter fruit
> Which Eve plucked from the tree,
> In Mary's fruit, see, all creation takes delight.

> The Tree of Life which was hidden in the midst of Paradise
> Grew in Mary and sprang from her;
> And in its shade creation dwelt,
> And it scattered its fruit for those both far and near.

> Mary wove a robe of glory and gave it to her forefather,
> Who had hidden himself among the trees.
> It clothed him and he grew chaste and acquired virtues:
> His wife pulled him down, but his daughter upheld him and
>   raised him a hero.

> Eve and the serpent dug the abyss and pulled Adam down;
> But Mary and the King set him right again,
> Drew him out and raised him from the deep
> By the hidden mystery which became manifest and gave life to
>   Adam.

> A Virgin produced a grape cluster whose wine was sweet,
> And by it were consoled from griefs
> Eve and Adam as they lamented;
> They tasted the Medicine of Life and by it were consoled from
>   their sorrows.[20]

These four stanzas are given as a complete hymn in one MS and I have quoted them in full since they introduce a number of other biblical images of Mary which are linked to the main typology of Mary the New Eve. In the last stanza of the anonymous hymn the fruit is specified as being the grape, because, typologically, the grape cluster which Jesus [Joshua] and Caleb brought back from the promised land on a pole is one of the well known images of Christ hanging upon the Cross, whose blood is the wine which gives life to all creatures. Mary may be seen not only as the Tree which bears the Fruit of Life but also as Paradise itself, as the garden of delight in which the Tree of Life grows. This is why in the traditional iconography of Paradise the Mother of God is shown enthroned, with her Son on her knees, amid the trees and flowers of Eden, alongside Abraham, with Lazarus in his bosom, and the other Patriarchs. The Thief, carrying the Cross, has entered Paradise, while the rest of humanity, led by the Apostles, waits outside. St Peter's keys hang useless at his side.

By his sin Adam had lost the garment of light which clothed him in Paradise, but Mary weaves in her womb the garment of flesh in which the Word clothes Himself, and which Adam in turn puts on by Baptism. 'As many of you as have been baptised into Christ have put on Christ' as the Apostle says. Another of this series of hymns describes Mary, Eve's daughter, as weaving the Robe of Glory as a gift for her mother, who had been clothed in leaves of shame.

The image of the robe woven by Mary is also used by St Ephrem in his *Hymns on Paradise*:

Naked, Adam was handsome;
   His diligent wife
Toiled to weave for him
   A garment of defilements:
The garden seeing him
   And finding him hideous, thrust him outside.
But a new tunic was made
   For him by Mary.
Clothed in this robe and according to the promise,
   The Thief was resplendent:
The garden, seeing Adam again in him,
   Embraced him.[21]

Finally on the imagery of Eve/Mary a passage from St Ephrem's *Diatessaron Commentary*:

Likewise Symeon says: 'You will make the sword pass'; the sword which protected paradise because of Eve has been taken away through Mary...Or perhaps: 'You will make the sword pass', (means) rather: 'You too will doubt', because 'she thought he was the gardener'.[22]

I include these two comments of St Ephrem because the second is one of the texts in which he appears to combine, or confuse, Mary Magdalen and Mary, the Mother of God.

In the traditional iconography of the Myrrhbearers one of them is always the Mother of God, and the Resurrection Dismissal Hymn in Tone 6 in the Byzantine *Octoichos* says quite clearly of the Risen Christ: 'You met the Virgin and granted life.' St John Chrysostom in his commentary on St Matthew's Gospel says:

And they saw Jesus first; and the sex that was most condemned was the first to enjoy the sight of the blessings, most showed its courage. When the disciples fled, the women were still there. But who were they? His Mother, for she is called *mother* of James.[23]

St Romanos, I think implies the same in the twelfth stanza of his

Kontakion for Good Friday, where he makes the dying Christ say to his Mother:

> Courage, Mother
> For you will be first to see me   come from the tomb;
> I am coming to show you   from what pains
>   I have ransomed Adam,
>   And how much I have sweated   for his sake;
>   I will reveal it to my friends,   showing them the proofs in my
>   hands;
> And then, Mother,   you will see Eve
>   Alive as before,   and you will cry out in joy;
>   'He has saved my forebears,   My Son and my God! [24]

This stanza is echoed remarkably closely in a popular Greek Easter song, still sung in the villages, which ends:

> And Christ spoke to her from up on the Cross:
> 'Quiet, Mother, don't cry; there's no point.
> 'And on Great Saturday then wait for me
> 'When the churches ring and the priests sing,
> 'Then you too, Mother, will have great joys'.

It is almost impossible to convey the feel of the Demotic in English.[25]

Severus of Antioch, in the early sixth century, in his 77th Homily, on the apparent discrepancies between the accounts of the Resurrection, says:

> The other Mary, whom we may properly believe to have been the Mother of God, because she did not remain distant from, the Passion, but stood by the Cross, as John recounted, to whom also the good tidings of joy were fitting, she who was the root of joy and who had gladly heard the greeting 'Hail [Rejoice], full of grace!', fulfilling the Lord's command, certainly announced the good news to the disciples. [26]

It is important to observe that while none of these writers confuses the Mother of God and Mary Magdalen, as St Ephrem does,[27] there is a clear tradition that the Mother of God was among the first, if not the first to see the Risen Christ.

3. The Mountain of God

Let us now leave the Garden of Eden for the Mountain of God, Sinai. Much of the typology of Mary centres on the affirmation that she is truly the Mother of God, that, though a mortal, she carried in her womb God the Word, the Second Person of the Holy Trinity. Perhaps the favourite Old Testament image that the Fathers have to express this doctrine is that of the Burning Bush, from chapter three of Exodus. It is not known when this passage is first applied to the

Mother of God. Cardinal Daniélou, in his edition of St Gregory of Nyssa's *Life of Moses*, suggests that St Gregory is the first to apply this passage to Mary, and adds that this 'attests the development of the theology of the Incarnation around the year 390'.[28] However the passage is already so used in the authentic work of St Ephrem at least twenty years earlier – St Ephrem died in 373 . In any case the use of the image seems to have been well-established more than half a century before the Council of Ephesus.

Here is how St Ephrem introduces the image in his *Commentary on the Diatessaron*, in a passage for which we only have the Syriac original:

> [The Son] was the coal which came to set fire to the thistles and thorns [an allusion to Genesis 3.18]. He dwelt in the womb and purified it; he hallowed the place of the pangs of childbirth and of curses [a further allusion to Genesis 3.16]. The flame which Moses saw moistened the bush, and rich fatness dripped from the flame, and like pure gold it appeared in the bramble bush which the fire entered yet the bush was not consumed, to make known the Living Fire which came in the last time, watered and moistened the Virgin's womb, and clothed itself in it, like the fire in the bush.[29]

The reference to the thorns of Genesis is not accidental, since the word used in both Hebrew and Syriac for the 'bush' means strictly a 'briar' or 'bramble', and the Greek word chosen by the LXX [*vatos*] also means 'bramble'. Philo in his comment on this passage stresses that the vatos is a thorny sort of plant.[30] St Gregory of Nyssa's account stresses the virginity of Mary:

> From this passage we are also taught about the mystery of the Virgin, from whom the light of the godhead shone out on human life through being born, leaving the burning bush intact, for the flower of virginity was not withered by giving birth. [31]

From the end of the fourth century this becomes one of the most common types of the mystery of the Incarnation and there is no need for extensive quotation. The paradox of the flame that does not devour leads easily to the other classic example, that of the Three Children in the fiery furnace, which is also used as a type of the Virgin's womb. Here the image is even more apposite, since Nabuchodonosor says that the mysterious fourth figure seen walking in the flames 'is like a son of God' [Dan.3.25 (92)]. An Irmos in Tone One for the seventh Ode of a Canon puts it like this:

> We faithful acknowledge you, Mother of God, to be a spiritual furnace; for as the Highly Exalted saved the Three children so He refashioned me, humanity, entirely in your womb, the God of

our Fathers, praised and highly exalted. [32]

The fire which becomes dew in the furnace also evokes the 'dew on the fleece' in the story of Gideon and in Psalm 71, one of the great Messianic psalms[33], and St Romanos, like others, combines the two types in the Prooemium to his Kontakion for December 26th, which survives as an independent troparion in the modern service books:

> Joseph was amazed when he contemplated an event beyond nature,
> And at your conceiving without seed, O Mother of God,
> He understood the rain on the fleece,
> The bush unconsumed by fire,
> Aaron's rod which blossomed,
> And your betrothed and guardian cried out to the priests:
> 'A Virgin bears a child, and after child-birth remains still a virgin'.[34]

St Proclus has an extraordinary development of this image of the fleece in his first Homily on the Mother of God. Mary, he says, is:

> The purest fleece of the heavenly rain, from which the Shepherd puts on the sheep... She alone is the bridge of God towards mankind. The dread loom-beam of the economy, on which the robe of the union [sc. of the two natures] was woven; whose weaver is the Holy Spirit; the spinner, the overshadowing Power from on high; the wool, the ancient fleece of Adam[35]; the thread, the immaculate flesh of the Virgin; the shuttle, the ineffable grace of Him who wore it; the craftsman, the Word who came to dwell through hearing.[36]

In Exodus chapter 19 God comes down upon Mt Sinai in the 'thick cloud' and this, linked to the words of the Archangel at the Annunciation: 'the power of the Most High will overshadow you', leads the Fathers to see in Mt Sinai itself a type of the Mother of God. Moreover it is on Mt Sinai that God utters the Ten Words, and as in both Greek and Hebrew the letter 'I' *yod* or *iota*, is used for the number ten, the symbolism is even more marked, since in both Greek and Hebrew the same letter is the initial letter of the name Jesus. This is how the Ethiopic *Weddāse Maryam*, or *Praise of Mary*, expresses it. The *Weddāse Maryam*, like the Coptic *Theotokia*, of which it is for the most part a translation, is a series of hymns in honour of the Mother of God for every day of the week, and forms part of the daily Office of both churches. Its origin is unknown, but it is popularly attributed to St Ephrem.

> The living Word of the Father, who came down upon Mount Sinai and gave the Law to Moses and covered the summit of the

mountain with fog and smoke, darkness and wind and the blast of trumpets, gave instruction to those who stood by in fear. Pray for us, holy Lady.

The Lover of mankind, who came down upon you in humility, O Mountain endowed with reason, became man through you without change, flesh like us, perfectly endowed with reason. Through the Spirit of Wisdom God dwelt upon her. He became perfect man, that He might save Adam and forgive his sin, place him once again in heaven and lead him back to his ancient throne, through the greatness of his mercy and pity. Pray for us, holy Lady.[37]

In terms of Sacred Geography the Mountain of God is not limited to the Sinai peninsula and there are three other mountains which are applied typologically to the Mother of God. The first is the mountain of Daniel 2.34,45. A stone cut without hands from the mountain smashes the great statue and itself becomes a great mountain.In the earlier period, for example in the third century commentary of Hippolytus, this is already seen as a Christological text, but the mountain from which the stone is hewn appears to be taken to mean the Father rather than Mary.[38] Certainly by the sixth century it was being applied to the Mother of God, as this Verse for Christmas attributed to St Romanos, but probably written later, indicates.

> You have been declared, O Virgin, to be the spiritual mountain
>   For from you was hewn the cornerstone
> Which the prophet saw destroying the image;
> This is He who smashed the might of the dread corrupter of
>   mankind:
>   Therefore we cry: 'Blessed are you who have been born, our
>   God, glory to you!'[39]

The second mountain with which the Mother of God is regularly identified, especially in the liturgical texts, is the 'Shaded, wooded mountain' of Habbakuk 3.3 [in the LXX], with its echo of Luke 1.35.[40] One reason for the popularity of this image is that the *Prayer of Habbakuk* forms part of the daily morning office in the Byzantine rite.

The third is the mountain of God in Psalm 67.16s. The AV translates a rare Hebrew word, which only occurs in these two verses in the Bible, by 'high'. Modern translators prefer 'many-peaked', or something similar, but the LXX, followed by the Vulgate, has 'curdled'. This is not as odd as it may appear, since the Hebrew word *gavnon* is certainly cognate with the word for 'curd' or 'cheese', *gʿvinah*.[41] In his later version from the Hebrew St Jerome put 'high', *excelsus*. The interpretation in this expression 'the Mountain of God is a fat mountain, a curdled mountain' was not easy, but it was taken to be an image of the Incarnation, because the growth of the foetus was believed by ancient medicine to be the result of the solidifying of the mother's blood by interaction with the male seed, a sort of 'curdling' process. Job uses precisely this image of himself: 'Did you not pour me out like milk, and curdle me like cheese?' [10.10 AV] The word the AV translates by 'cheese' is *g^e vinah*.[42] In his Kontakion for Good Friday St Romanos puts this image into the mouth of Christ as he addresses his Mother from the Cross:

Do not declare the day of my Passion bitter;
>Because it was for it that I, the sweet one, came down from heaven like the manna
>Not onto Mount Sinai, but into your womb;
Within it I was curdled, as David prophesied;
>Understand the 'curdled mountain', noble Lady:
>For it is I; for being the Word I became flesh in you:
In flesh I suffer, and in flesh I save;
>Do not weep then, Mother, but rather cry with joy:
>'Willingly He accepts the passion,
>>My Son and my God!'[43]

As the French editor of Romanos said that he had not found this exegesis anywhere else, though it is in fact found in the liturgical texts, most of which are later than Romanos and could ultimately derive from this Kontakion, I will give one example from a Lenten Canon by St Joseph the Hymnographer:

We beseech you, O Virgin unwedded, royal chariot, bright cloud, mountain most rich, curdled mountain: heal the passions of our souls.[44]

St Romanos seems almost to suggest that the Word comes down like sweet milk, which is then 'curdled' into cheese. There is no way of knowing whether Romanos who was Syrian by birth and certainly knew the works of St Ephrem, could have known the *Odes of Solomon*, but the ideas are not entirely dissimilar to those in the extraordinary nineteenth Ode, which contains what must be one of the earliest references to the Mother of God, and without which no survey, however superficial, of Mary in Eastern Christian Literature would be complete. The following is the translation by the latest editor of the text, R.H. Charlesworth,[45] with a few alterations.

1. A cup of milk was offered me,
And I drank it in the sweetness of the Lord's kindness.

2. The Son is the cup,
And the Father is He who was milked,

And the one who milked Him is the Holy Spirit.

3. Because His breasts were full
And He wished that His milk should be generously outpoured.

4. The Holy Spirit opened Her bosom,
And mixed the milk of the two breasts of the Father.

5. And gave the mixture to the world without their knowing,
But those who receive it in its fullness are those on the right   hand.

6. The Virgin's womb enclosed it,
And she received conception and gave birth.

7. And the Virgin became a Mother through many mercies.

8. And she was in labour and gave birth to the Son without pain.
Because it did not occur without purpose.

9. And she did not seek a midwife,
Because He caused her to give life.

10. She brought Him forth as a strong man by His own will,
And she gave birth according to the manifestation,
And acquired with great power.

11. And loved with redemption,
And guarded with kindness,
And made manifest with grandeur.

Hallelujah!

It is beyond the scope of this paper to try to unravel the many problems posed by this very early Christian hymn.[46] Similar imagery of the 'milk of the Father' is found in Clement of Alexandria, and I suspect that one scriptural source may be Psalm 109.3, which in the LXX and the Syriac, though not in the Hebrew, reads: 'From the womb before the morning star I have begotten you'.[47] The milk is at once the Word and the word: the Virgin Mother is at once Mary and the Church. Father Robert Murray writes of the 'mutually typical relationship of Mary and the church' as follows: 'The Church and Mary are interwoven as types, and this relationship becomes a principle of patristic theology'.[48] St Ephrem in a comment on Deuteronomy 18.5 writes:

> He [Jesus] replaced Joshua the son of Nun by John, who was a virgin, and entrusted to him Mary, his church, as Moses entrusted his flock to Joshua. [49]

4. Mary as Tabernacle and Ark

The Mountain of God in Psalm 67 is the 'mountain where God is pleased to dwell, His abode to the end', and the Targum specifically identifies it with Mount Moriah, the Temple Mount. Mary is God's dwelling, the Holy City of Jerusalem, Holy Sion, the Temple itself.

She is the outer Gate of the new Temple, which faces the East, the point from which the Sun comes from His chamber, another type of the Mother of God, like a bridegroom and rejoices like a strong man [Ps. 19.5]. The Gate is shut because the Lord God of Israel has entered by it [Ez. 44.1-2].

And so finally I would like simply to put before you some of the many types of Mary in connection with the Temple, the dwelling place of God among men. In all these types Mary is seen as the one who contains or bears something greater than herself. The Sunday Theotokia in the Coptic office sums up the essentials of this typology:

1. O blessed among women, you are rightly called the Second Tent, which is called the Holy of Holies, and within which are the Tables of the Covenant written by the finger of God. They signify for us in advance the Iota, the name of salvation, Jesus. He it is who received flesh in you without change and has become the Mediator of a New Covenant. Through the sprinkling of his holy Blood He has purified those who believe into a people that He justifies.
   Refrain: Because of this everyone exalts you as truly the ever-holy Mother of God. Therefore we ask that through your prayers we may obtain mercy at the hands of Him who loves mankind.

2. The Ark which was covered with gold on every side was made of imperishable woods. It was made as a sign beforehand of God the Word, who became man without separation. He is one from two, perfect godhead without corruption, consubstantial with the Father and, consubstantial with us according to the economy, sacred humanity without confusion, which He took within you, O spotless one, and was united with it hypostatically.

3. The Mercy-seat which rested upon the Cherubim forms an icon of God the Word who took flesh in you, O most pure, without change. He became a purification of sins and a pardoner of iniquities.

4. You are the Jar of pure gold in the midst of which is concealed the Manna, the Bread of life which came down from heaven and gave life to the world.

5. You are the Lampstand of pure gold which bears the Lamp which burns forever, the unapproachable Light of the world from the unapproachable Light; true God of true God, who took flesh in you without change. By his coming He has enlightened us who dwell in darkness and the shadow of death. He has directed our feet in the way of peace through the communion of His holy mysteries.

6. You are the Censer of pure gold which bears the Coal of blessed

fire, which was taken from the altar and takes away our iniquities. He is God the Word who took flesh of you and offered Himself as a sweet savour to God his Father.

7. Hail Mary, fair dove who gave birth for us to God the Word. You are the sweet-scented Flower which blossomed from the root of Jesse. Aaron's rod, which flowered without planting and watering, is a type of you who gave birth to Christ our God in truth without seed of man and yet are Virgin.

All the types in this catalogue stress either Mary's Virginity or her role in the Economy as Mother of God, Theotokos, and there is no need for detailed comments. On the other hand these types are the starting points for the use of a number of other passages of Scripture as types of the Mother of God. Thus if Christ is the coal on the altar, then Mary is also the tongs which the Seraph uses to bring the coal to purify the lips of the Prophet, and she is thus brought into close connection with the Eucharist, since in all the Eastern tradition the burning coal typifies the Eucharistic Bread, so much so that the Greek word for the spoon used to distribute Communion to the people is *lavis*, which does not mean 'spoon' at all, but 'tongs'. [50]

If Christ is the Mercy seat who rests upon the Cherubim, then Mary is herself the Cherubim throne, the *Merkavah*, and all the passages which refer to it refer to her, notably Ezekiel chapter 1, Psalms 79.1 and 98.1 together with a number of others. This is how one of the Syriac hymns to the Mother of God puts it:

Your place, my Son, is higher than all,
And as You willed You made me a place for Yourself.
Heaven is too small for Your glory;
Yet I, a poor girl, carry You.
Let Ezekiel come and see You on my knees,
And let him kneel and adore You, and recognise that it was You
Whom he saw there, high upon the Cherubim,
Above the Chariot, and let him call me blessed
On account of Him whom I bear.

At me the Chariot marvelled,
For I carry its rider.
See, the Cherubim cry out with fear:
'Blessed is Your glory from Your place!'
See, Your place is with me, and my bosom is Your dwelling;
Your tabernacle is on my knees; and the throne of Your greatness
My supporting arms; instead of wheels my fingers
Form your Chariot; like it I will cry out:
'Blessed are You from Your place'. [51]

It was no doubt with these passages from Isaias 6 and Ezekiel 1, among others, in mind that St Cosmas, in his Canon for Good Friday, called Mary 'Greater in honour than the Cherubim and beyond compare more glorious than the Seraphim'.

Time does not allow me to go any further, though, as you will realise, I have only scratched the surface of the subject; for Mary is also 'Jacob's Ladder', by which God came down to earth, 'the house of God' and the 'gate of heaven' [Gen. 28. 12-17], the 'beauty of Jacob' [Ps. 46.4], the 'Queen', who stands at the King's right hand [Ps. 44.10], the 'ship' which brings the wealth of Tharsis [III Kings 10.22], 'undergirded', as an Ethiopian hymn says, 'with the ropes of the Trinity which cannot be separated', the 'Red Sea', which again became impassable after Israel God's Son had passed through it [Ex. 14.28s].

There may perhaps be some who find this imagery extravagant and inappropriate, but on the one hand, it is only the fulfilment of her own prophecy in the *Magnificat* and on the other, all the types and images, as in the icon of the Hodegetria, point from Mary to her Son. As she herself is made to say by the Syrian poet I quoted just now, 'let him [Ezekiel] call me blessed *on account of Him I bear*'. If the Eastern tradition of devotion to Mary as we meet it in the texts teaches anything, it is that there is no authentic devotion to Mary which is not firmly Christocentric. All Scripture points towards Christ, including the images which typify his Mother, who bore in her womb the fire of the Godhead without being destroyed, who 'without corruption gave birth to God the Word, and whom as truly the Mother of God we magnify'. Or, because I would like to end with one of my favourite verses from my own patron, St Ephrem, from one of his hymns for the Nativity:

Your Mother is a cause of wonder.   The Lord entered her
And became a servant.   The Word entered
And fell silent within her.   The Thunder entered her
And made no sound.   The Shepherd of all entered,
In her became the Lamb: He came out and bleated. 52

Notes

1. *Omnis scriptura diuinitus inspirata utilis est ad docendum.* Note in the previous verse the reference to 'sacred writings', which must refer to the Old Testament. The fact that current critical fashion does not consider St Paul to be the author of the Pastorals does not affect the argument. They are part of Holy Scripture.

2. *PG* 56:110.

3. 'The Mother of God in Holy Scripture', in *The Mother of God. A Symposium*, ed. E. Mascall (London 1949), 13. Dr Thornton is in fact more concerned with the New Testament than with the Old.

4. 'The Reasonableness of Typology' in *Essays in Typology* (London 1957), 14.

5. Op cit 21.

6. 'Panagia' in *The Mother of God*, 35.

7. *Demonstration of the Apostolic Preaching*, 33. This work is cited from the edition of the Armenian version in *PO* 12 (No. 161). The English version opposite the text is quite unreliable, and the appended French version, with valuable notes by Père Tixeront, is to be preferred.

8. 37.8 St Romanos' Kontakia are cited according to the Oxford edition by Maas and Trypanis. Their numbering and often their titles are quite different from those in the edition in *Sources Chrétiennes*.

9. Op cit 32.

10. *Diat.* II.2. References are given according to Dom Louis Leloir's French version in *Sources Chrétiennes* No. 121 (Paris 1966). The passage quoted only exists in the Armenian version (*CSCO* 137). Dom Louis has recently announced the discovery of a number of new leaves of the original Syriac, but I was not able to make use of them in preparing this paper. Dom Louis' own Latin versions of the Armenian and Syriac are often closer to the originals than his French version.

11. *Nat.* I:14-16 (*CSCO* 187). The authentic works of St Ephrem are all cited from the editions by Dom Edmund Beck in *CSCO*.

12. *PG* 65: 756A. Cf Mat 13.44.

13. See 'L'Annonciation à Marie dans la liturgie syrienne' by Dom Théophane Ardans in *L'Orient Syrien* Vol. IV (1959), 468.

14. See 'Le thème de la Perle chez Jacques de Saroug' by Père Francois Graffin in *L'Orient Syrien* Vol. XII (1967), 362s. This idea is used in a most interesting way by St Romanos in his Kontakion for the Annunciation (36.12), in which Mary says to Joseph of Gabriel's visit:

   A winged being came to me gave me gifts of betrothal
   Pearls for my ears;

He hung his words like rings upon my ears.

15. Sunday Resurrection Canon, Ode 8, Theotokion.

16. *Pearl* I.4 (*CSCO* 154). Morris's version, re-published in the *Nicene and Post-Nicene Fathers*, for some reason omits the word 'Mary'.

17. *Pearl* III.2.

18. *Dem.* 33.

19. Menaion, 18 February Ode 9, Theotokion.

20. *Hymni de Beata Maria* I.10-14. These hymns were published by Lamy, *Sancti Ephraem Hymni et Sermones* Vol II (Malines 1886), 517-642. Most, if not all, of them are not by St Ephrem, but they are probably not much later.

21. *Parad.* IV.5 (*CSCO* 174).

22. *Diat.* II.17.

23. *PG* 88:778.

24. 19.12.

25. For example, the Greek uses the popular *papades* for 'priests' and the familiar *manoula* for 'mother'.

26. *PO* 16:810. The greeting in Greek means both 'Hail' and 'Rejoice', and the references are to Luke 1:28 and Matt 28:9. According to St Matthew only two Maries visit the tomb, Mary Magdalen and the 'other' Mary. The statement by John Wenham in *The Easter Enigma* (Exeter 1983), 135 '.. some scholars are even advocating an appearance of Jesus to his mother in spite of the fact that for many centuries the New Testament and early Christian tradition had been gleaned meticulously in search of any scrap of information which might honour the Blessed Virgin, without finding any trace of an appearance to her after the resurrection, such as was granted to the "other" Mary', only shows his ignorance of Christian tradition, whether early or late. St Ignatius Loyola, apparently quite independently, holds that the Lord appeared first to His Mother. See the beginning of the fourth week of the *Exercises*.

27. A number of reasons have been given for this and I would like to put forward one that I do not think has been suggested before. St Ephrem's commentary is based on Tatian's lost harmony of the Gospels, the *Diatessaron*, though various later versions are extant. The problem is that we cannot be sure how accurately they represent the original. One complete version is in Arabic. In this version the four accounts of the first Easter morning are cunningly woven together to make one more or less coherent account. The striking thing is that, following St Matthew's account, only two names are mentioned in the first part of the harmony, Mary Magdalen and the 'other' Mary. One of the verses which the harmoniser has sacrificed is John 20.1, and with it the mention of Mary Magdalen. The next sixteen

verses are retained, but, and this is the crucial point, *without* verse 1, they could refer *either* to Mary Magdalen or to the 'other' Mary. I suggest therefore that the original reason for the confusion in St Ephrem was that in his *Diatessaron* it was not in fact stated that the Mary of John 20.2-17 was Mary Magdalen; it could equally well have been the 'other' Mary, who, as Severus of Antioch remarks 'may properly be believed to have been the Mother of God'. In his fourth hymn on the Resurrection St Ephrem speaks of an appearance to the Mother of God:

In the month of Nisan our Lord came down from on high,
And Mary received Him. Again in Nisan
He was raised and ascended, and Mary saw Him again.

28. *Vie de Moïse*, SC Iter (Paris 1968), 119 n 3.

29. *Diat.* I.25.

30. The stress on the idea of 'moisture' is also found in St Gregory of Nyssa [*Life of Moses*, I.20]. Philo says much the same [*Life of Moses*, I.65], while Josephus [*Ant* II.266] stresses that the bramble retained its greenness and its fruit-laden branches. In Jewish tradition the bramble symbolises the suffering people of God. This idea is found both in Philo, and in the Rabbinic tradition. Rashi's comment is: 'A thornbush - not any other kind, in accordance with "I will be with him in trouble" [Ps 91(90).15].'.

31. *Life of Moses* II.21.

32. The LXX at Daniel 3.25(92) has 'the appearance of the fourth, likeness of an angel', but Theodotion, whose version of Daniel replaced that of the LXX in Church use, has 'like a son of God'. The Aramaic has *bar-elahin*, literally 'a son of the gods', that is, in accordance with normal Semitic idiom, 'a divine (or angelic) being'. The AV, clearly influenced by christological considerations, has 'the Son of God'.

33. The LXX here has 'and He will come down like rain upon a fleece'. The Hebrew word translated 'fleece' is *gēz*, from the √*gāzaz* 'to shear'. The word is rare, and only occurs here, at Deut.18.4, Job 31.20 and, in the plural, Amos 7.1. In Deut and Job it means 'sheep shearings', but here and in Amos probably 'mown grass', or perhaps 'grass ready for mowing'. The word used in the story of Gideon in Judges 6, and only there in the Hebrew Bible, is the cognate *gizzah*. St Jerome, in his version of the Psalter *iuxta Hebraeos*, takes the Hebrew to mean 'fleece', though one cannot always trust St Jerome not to be influenced by theology. The Targum expands with 'like grass sheared off by the locust'.

34. 37, Prooemium.

35. *PG* 65:681. The word he uses is *kodion*, and this phrase, 'Adam's fleece' is found in the Byzantine service books as a title of the Moth-

er of God. For example in the Sunday Canon of the Mother of God in Tone 1:

Hail Holy One, Adam's fleece, from you came forth the Shepherd, the highly-exalted, truly clothed in human nature.

36. *PG* 65:681. There is a remarkable echo of this in the Ethiopian *Anaphora of the Mother of God*, where we find the following:

O Virgin full of praise, with what and with what likeness shall we compare you? You are a loom, for Emmanuel clothed Himself from you in the garment of ineffable flesh. The warp was made from Adam's flesh; your flesh was the weft; the shuttle the Word Himself, Jesus Christ; the beam from above the overshadowing of God from on high, and the Weaver is the Holy Spirit.

37. W.M. Tuesday 8-9. I use the edition published by De Lacy O'Leary in 1923; for the *Weddase Maryam* that by the late Père Velat in *PO* 34 (Paris 1966).

38. *In Danielem* II.13. cf Hippolyte, *Commentaire sur Daniel*, SC 14 (Paris 1947), 144-6.

39. 83.4. In +P. Maas and C. A. Trypanis *Sancti Romani Melodi Cantica Dubia* (Berlin 1970). For the question of authenticity cf p. XIII.

40. The preceding verse in the LXX contains the phrase 'In the middle of two living beings you will be known', which, combined with Isa 1.3, is the source for the tradition of the ox and the ass of the Nativity.

41. The RSV with most moderns treats the Hebrew *elohim* as equivalent to an adjective meaning 'great' and translates *har-elohim* as 'Mighty mountain'. The Cambridge Psalter takes the same view. The Targum elaborates greatly, but renders the word *gavnunim* by 'hump-backed'. The mountains are thus unsuitable for God's service, and so are to be rejected in favour of Mount Moriah.

42. The LXX and St Jerome both translate 'mountain of Bashan' in the Psalm by 'fat mountain', not unintelligently, since Bashan in the Bible is often a symbol of fertility. This makes very good sense coupled with 'curdled'. The references in the liturgical texts to the Mother of God as the 'fat mountain' are also to this Psalm.

43. 19.6.

44. Tuesday of the Second Week, Ode 9, First Canon, Theotokion.

45. J. H. Charlesworth, *The Odes of Solomon*, (Oxford 1973), 81-4. Cf also J. Labourt and P. Batiffol, *Les Odes de Salomon* (Paris) 1911, 74-8.

46. The last stanzas are particularly difficult and Batiffol indulges in extensive emendation, on the basis of a reconstructed, supposed, Greek original. In Syriac there is a play on words in stanza 9 because in Syriac the words for 'midwife', *haytâ*, and 'give life', *a'hiy*, are

closely related. We find similar ideas in the *Protoevangelium of James.* In verse 11 there may be an allusion to Psalm 18.5 and possibly to Daniel 10.11, though Professor Antoine Guillaumont believes that the phrase 'like a man' simply means '*activement*'. 'Manifestation' may be an allusion to Gabriel's message and also to the visible nature of the birth. For a similar use of 'manifestation' one might venture to compare the passage in the so-called *Bazaar of Heraclides* of Nestorius. Cf *Le Livre d'Heraclide de Damas,* (Paris 1910), 173. 'Acquired' is the same word used in Proverbs 8.22 and also by Eve in Gen 4.1. If, as Charlesworth suggests, 'Power' is used, as it was in the very early Church, to refer to God, then the link with Genesis 4 is even clearer. Indeed it might be possible to add Ode 19 to the dossier of early examples of the Eve/Mary typology

47. The Syriac, in fact, does not have the words 'before the morning star', but it does have 'from the womb'.

48. R. Murray, *Symbols of Church and Kingdom,* (Cambridge 1973), 144.

49. *Diat.* XII.5.

50. Theodoret in his *Eranistes,* written around 447, quotes what he claims is a discourse on Psalm 22 by Hippolytus in which the Ark of the Covenant is seen as linked to the typology of the Mother of God: 'And the Ark of incorruptible woods was the Saviour. .... For the Lord was without sin from the Virgin and the Holy Spirit, within and without covered with the purest gold of the Word of God.' *PG* 83:88. Mary is also compared to the Veil of the Temple in both Syriac and Ethiopic texts. Sometimes the expression used is 'Veil of Light'. In a number of Ethiopic texts this image is also linked to the Eucharist. Thus in a prayer of the Empress Helena we read: 'My Lady, Veil of joy and purity, grant that I may enter the inner sanctuary of Him whom you bore, for I hope to receive Communion of the Mysteries of Him whom you nursed, and long to share in the Holy Gifts of Him whom you nourished at your breasts.' In view of this the Epiclesis of the Ethiopian *Anaphora of the Mother of God* is interesting: 'May the Gates of glory be opened, the Veil of light drawn back, and may the Holy Spirit come and overshadow this bread and this cup, and make them the Body and Blood of our Lord and Saviour, Jesus Christ.'

51. *Hymni de Beata Maria,* VII. 4-5.

52. *Nat.* XI.6.

The convertible relation:
an exercise in revisionary theology

Ian Davie, Esq. M.A.
Roman Catholic, Ampleforth College, York

Preamble

1. It is not we who imagine – or can imagine – God, but God who imagines (images) us, and since what God imagines, God creates, then the difference between God's imagining us and our being imagined will be the difference between God-language, where utterance and realisation are always coincident, and our language, where they are not. None the less, there will be a relation of analogy between the two – not a *resemblance-relation*, as though there were some common quality to be picked out, but, rather, a *relational resemblance* – i.e. of inverse analogy between ourselves-as-imagined and God-as-Imaginer.

2. So, when we speak of God as Father, for example, we do not suppose that God is *like* a human father: we do not claim that characterics of human fatherhood can be predicated of God. On the contrary, we employ the *inverse analogy*[1] of God as the Source of all paternity, (and, by parity of reasoning, of God as the Source of all maternity), and, in doing so, we *reverse* the direction of the analogy – from the anthropomorphic to the theomorphic. In short, given *that* God exists, instead of analogizing directly from the human to the divine, we analogize inversely from the divine to the human: that is to say, the idea of God (e.g. as 'that than which a greater cannot be conceived', to take Anselm's formulation in the *Proslogion*) governs our analogies and not our analogies the idea of God.

3. I take it as axiomatic that the 'what' of God's being cannot be known, except by God. When we are theologizing about the Trinity and the Incarnation, these mysteries transcend our comprehension, *ex hypothesi*, so there is not much point in lamenting the inadequacy of language to encompass what is beyond it. Yet, although these mysteries transcend our comprehension, they cannot be wholly beyond our apprehension. When we say that God is Love, for example, the term 'Love' cannot be out of all relation to what we mean by 'Love', humanly speaking. What, then, are we doing when we presume to speak of such mysteries? I think the answer is that, whether we speak as philosophers or as theologians, we are, as rational beings, under an obligation to ensure that terms are used consistently. For example, if we say that God is Pure Act, and if this means that there is no potentiality in God (or that there is nothing which God might be

doing that God is not already doing), it would seem to follow that, since sonhood is potential fatherhood, there is a sense, as yet unexplored, in which fatherhood can be predicated of the Son.

4. Although we cannot, of course, know what it is like to be God, we can know what God is like, on the basis of our belief that we are made in God's image. As Wittgenstein says, 'the human body is the best picture of the human soul'[2]; if so, it is only by cherishing the human body as the image of God that we can begin to understand what is meant by saying 'God is Love'. For however much that image may be defaced, it is not wholly lost. As Hopkins says:

> There lives the dearest freshness deep down things
> ...*because* the Holy Ghost over the bent
> World broods with warm breast and with ah! bright wings. [3]

Although we cannot, as creatures, speak God-language, the question which should occupy us is not whether we can speak God-language, but whether God can speak *our* language, and for that question to be answered in the affirmative, what is required is a radical revision of our idea of God: our preconceptions have to be overturned. We have to think of God, not only as the Source of all paternity and the Source of all maternity, but as the Form of Filiality, and hence as capable of being incarnate. But, granted that God can, and does, speak our language, then, if humankind is indeed made in God's image – male and female – the genders which distinguish us must surely be divinely prepossessed by the engendering power of the God who confers them upon us?

5. In a recent article in *The Tablet*,[4] Charles Davis contends that the maleness of Jesus is no more relevant to his redemptive role than the colour of his hair. On the contrary, I want to say that everything contributing to his maleness is relevant, every particle of his body, from the hair of his head to the genes that determine its colour. If the chromosomes that determine his gender are not relevant, then Jesus becomes a random product of the genetic lottery; but to think of Jesus like this would entail abandoning the idea of divine intentionality – the explanatory force of God's having a purpose – and this in turn would nullify the claim of Jesus to have privileged access to that intentionality. But on what other basis can we ascribe divinity to him? Furthermore, Charles Davis maintains that the employment of physical generation, or procreation, as the basic analogy in our conceptualization of the Trinity, is a crude mistake. If this were so, it would indeed be a crude mistake, but the basic analogy is not of *pro*-creation, but of its inverse, the *proto*-creative engendering power of God which makes itself visible in the specific genders, both of the divine Humanity and of our humanity.

6. What is at issue here is the meaning of Incarnation as visibility, audibility, tangibility – in short, communicatability. Is God who is, by definition, the ultimate determining factor, to be denied the use of his creation, at all levels, in the engendering of his Son under the conditions of our humanity? Is gender of no account in the incarnational transaction between divine fatherhood and human motherhood? However strong the prejudice Charles Davis may entertain against ascribing gender distinctions to God, it is not a prejudice which God seems to share. If God, who is Spirit, is made visible in Jesus, as Soul is made visible in Body, and Energy in Mass (Matter), then the engendering power of the godhead as paternal-filial-maternal will be made visible in the specific genders of its exponents, Jesus and Mary. That is my theme.

Argument

7. In one of my most cherished books, Henry Adams' *Mont Saint Michel and Chartres*, the Virgin Mary is recorded as having said of Jesus, in relation to herself, 'We are Love'.[5] I want to persuade you that the Love between them is expressible as that power by which the Mother-Son relation is convertible to the Father-Daughter relation, and in attempting to do so I shall treat Dante's invocation of Mary – *Virgine Madre, figlia del tuo Figlio* [6]– not as poetic hyperbole, but as a *theologoumenon* ('A deduction reached by theological reasoning from other accepted religious truths or the expression of another form of a religious truth.' cf. John McHugh, *The Mother of Jesus in the New Testament*, London, 1975, p.309). I do not know whether Dante could have been influenced by the theology of the great Andalusian Sufi, Ibn 'Arabi, but I find it very remarkable that the same insight should have been preserved in several Islamic texts, from Al–Hallaj (in the 10th century) to Ibn 'Arabi (in the 13th). This is the more remarkable when one considers the Islamic declaration – 'God is neither Begetting nor Begotten', asserted, as it is, in opposition to the Christian declaration – 'God is both Begetting and Begotten'. What is denied as attributable to God is affirmed as attributable to Mary. Since Mary is a creature, this is only to be expected: what is unexpected is that Mary should find herself on both sides of the great divide postulated by Islamic orthodoxy. It would seem, then, that something approaching a doctrine of incarnation enters Islamic (Sufi/Shia) theology through contemplation of the mystery of Maryam. Islam, it should be noted has never questioned the truth of the Virgin Birth, and Jesus is always 'the Son of Maryam'. Indeed, Maryam appeared in a vision to Ibn 'Arabi (in Mecca) as the figure of the divine Sophia, the eternal correlate of the Logos, and he quotes the riddling *qasida* attributed to his spiritual master, Al Hallaj: 'My mother gave birth to her father' (omm abī–

hā).[7] The speaker is Jesus and what the paradox seeks to articulate is the mystery of the Woman whose function it is to be the creatrix of her Creator. Not that Mary is 'Mother of God' reduplicatively (i.e. not that she is the Mother of God-as-originative Father), but that she is Mother in the temporal order of her creator in the eternal order: in short, that she is Mother of God incarnate.

8. But before I go on to draw out the implications of what I call 'the convertible relation', I should like to consider the relation which seems to me to hold between Meaning and Understanding, since that relation bears directly on the central relation which is my true subject. Meaning and Understanding are correlatives. To say that 'Meaning' implies at least the possibility of 'Understanding' is simply to say that the response which we call 'Understanding' is implied by the intelligibility which we call 'Meaning'. As the meaning of 'God' when fully understood, implies the existence of God (Anselm's argument), to say that this meaning is instantiated is to assert that the nature of God is revealed in this meaning. And how could such a meaning be instantiated, unless by someone who embodied the meaning – the Word-made-flesh? But if this were so, only the response of faith could reveal it to be so – faith that had found understanding in response to the meaning so declared.

9. Allow me to repeat the argument in order to make its application clear.

(i) The meaning of 'God' implies the *existence* of God. (This is the core of the Anselmian argument, the strategy of which is to make the meaning explicit, so that it *is* understood, and there is then no question left.)

(ii) The revelation of God's *nature* turns on a comparable relation of complementarity between Meaning and Understanding. The Meaning of God's Self-disclosure, the Logos, is, we believe, made flesh and blood in Jesus, but divine self-disclosure is made conditional on the response of creaturely faith – of faith-in-search-of-understanding (Anselm's *Fides quaerens intellectum*). And that response finds its perfect vehicle in the Annunciation-experience of Mary.

The application of this argument will now be evident: it is simply that the response of *our* faith-in-search-of-understanding rests on Mary's prior faith-in-search-of-understanding, for Mary is to Jesus as Understanding is to Meaning, Wisdom to Word, Sophia to Logos. In short, the relation of Meaning to Understanding in respect of God's *existence* is paralleled in respect of God's *nature*, where Meaning corresponds to Logos, and Understanding to Sophia, in the eternal order, and to their embodiments, Jesus and Mary, in the temporal order.

10. A further philosophical point needs to be made. 'Jesus Christ is God' is not a sentence of the subject–predicate type. 'Divinity' is no more a predicate than 'existence' is a predicate: it is, rather, a function of the subject's knowledge. If to say 'Jesus Christ is God' *means* that the knowledge to which Jesus lays claim is true, then clearly 'God' is not a predicate but rather a function which is satisfied by a truth–value which, in this case, is the knowledge to which Jesus lays claim. But if the divinity of Jesus consists in the *truth* of his claim to a unique filial relationship with his heavenly Father, then the Virginal Conception of Jesus is an implication of this claim. That is to say, if the identity of the earthly Jesus depends on the truth of his self–identification with the Father (e.g. in such sayings as 'I and the Father are one' and 'Whoever has seen me has seen the Father') that self–identification would, if true, depend on his earthly life being the issue of a direct transaction between divine fatherhood and human motherhood. And the only evidence we could have for its being true would be the testimony of Mary (as preserved by St Luke). So here again we have a case of mutual implication – by which I mean no more than that you cannot have one without the other.

11. Similarly for dogma: you cannot have one dogma without another: you can't pick and choose, because 'Revealed Religion', as Newman said, 'is one comprehensive moral fact'.[8] Thus the dogmas of the Immaculate Conception of Mary, the Virginal Conception of Jesus, the Resurrection of Jesus and the Assumption of Mary, imply one another and form a system, as it were, of mutually supporting truths. As Wittgenstein says: 'When we first begin to *believe* anything, what we believe is not a single proposition, it is a whole system of propositions. (Light dawns gradually over the whole.) It is not single axioms that strike me as obvious, it is a system in which consequences and premises give one another *mutual* support.' Or again, 'The child learns to believe a host of things – i.e. it learns to act according to those beliefs. Bit by bit there forms a system of what is believed, and in that system some things stand unshakeably fast and some are more or less liable to shift. What stands fast does so, not because it is intrinsically obvious or convincing: it is, rather, held fast by what lies around it.'[9]

12. Our dogmas stand fast: what shifts is the meaning of the terms in which dogma is stated: particular terms, like Hypostasis and Person, and framework terms, like Nature and Revelation. If Revealed Religion is one comprehensive moral fact, it must be an immensely inclusive fact; and as its medium is Incarnation, so must Incarnation be understood inclusively. Indeed, I should like to suggest that there is some merit in thinking of Incarnation, not simply as a determinate event marked by the Nativity, but as a preparatory

process leading up to that event. In short, I want the term 'Incarnation' to embrace Mary as well as Jesus, without any suggestion that Mary is supernaturally conceived, or anything like that. If Incarnation-as-event is pictured in metaphors of descent ('He came down from heaven'), Incarnation-as-process would be pictured in metaphors of ascent. That is to say, if we can think of the eternal as temporalised in Jesus, we can equally well think of the temporal as eternalised in Mary. Mary would then be placed at the evolutionary summit: she would be the culminating point of natural perfection in a preparatory process which started with Creation. Though the Word's being made flesh in Jesus would differ from the manner of Wisdom's being made flesh in Mary, the difference would correspond exactly to that already noted – between a determinate event in history and a process co-extensive with the unfolding of human history from the Beginning.

13. Let us, then, suppose that there are two trajectories: one running from without to within – from God as Transcendent Cause, through Creation, to God as Immanent Cause; and the other, running from within to without – from God as Immanent Cause, through Incarnation, to God as Transcendent Cause. The divine Transcendence (signifying the First Person) and the divine Immanence (signifying the Third Person) would then be oriented towards each other incarnationally, and the three categories – Transcendence, Immanence, and Incarnation – would form the categorical basis on which three dispositions could be ascribed to the godhead: these dispositions would be designated 'paternal', 'filial', and 'maternal', and their Subjects would be the Source of Paternity (First Person), the Form of Filiality (Second Person), and the Source of Maternity (Third Person). If, then, God is Love in virtue of internal relations of co–inherence in the godhead, the First Person (the *wherefrom*) would signify God's Originative Love, the Third Person (the *whereby*) would signify God's Responsive Love, and the Second Person would signify both God's Unitive Love *ad intra* (the *wherein*), and God's Redemptive Love *ad extra* (the *whereto*).

14. St. John attributes the motivation of Incarnation to God's Love: 'God so loved the World.' Yet for God the Son to be incarnate, God must first create the means by which God is born, and 'the whereby' of such creation is the Holy Spirit. So, from within the natural order, the Holy Spirit draws out, through the desire of countless generations of mothers, the creaturely perfection which provides the means, and the process of parturition, which starts with Creation itself, culminates in the Immaculate Conception of Mary. The notion that Mary is scripturally marginal, and that the dogmas associated with her are dispensable accretions, has no basis what-

soever. The Old Testament Daughter of Zion is none other than the Mother of the Messiah foretold by the prophets, and the Mother of the Messiah is none other than the Woman of Apocalypse xii, the Heavenly Virgin Daughter. Indeed, the whole history of mankind is inscribed in the lineage of Mary. Of 'the Woman crowned with stars' (Apoc. xii,1), Austin Farrer writes: 'Hers is the womb from which the Messiah, or his kingdom, is to be born, and her position in the firmament may signify that her son's birth is into heaven, and takes effect in his enthronement there. But who is she? She is that Eve who in all history and in all generations of her race has been travailing to bring forth the Christ and the age to come... She is actualized in each of those mothers whose childbearing lay in a line towards Christ... Yet the person of the Woman is not simply confined within the single body pregnant at any given time with messianic destiny. The whole community is Eve, and in Rachel or in Mary travails to bring forth. So the prophets had depicted the Daughter of Zion, in labour to bring forth her salvation. (Isaiah xxvi, 16ff; Micah iv, 9ff; Jeremiah iv, 31). Whereas the desired birth may be metaphorical for the prophets, it is actual for the Christian seer: Zion brings forth salvation in bringing forth a saviour, first from the womb, and after from the tomb.'[10]

15. If the spirit is the 'whereby' of the Son's generation in eternity and in time – *per modum generationis* – it performs a maternal function, despite the opinion held by Aquinas to the contrary – viz. that 'In the generation of the Word, there is no relationship to motherhood, but only to fatherhood.'[11] But this is not to say that the Holy Spirit is God the Mother, for that ascription would nullify Mary's entitlement to be called 'Mother of God': it is, rather, to characterize the Spirit as the Source of Maternity, not as bearing, but as bringing to birth, as enabling motherhood, as the power of parturition at all levels – physical, conceptual, spiritual. The Spirit broods over the deep at the birth of the world, hatching it, as it were; the Spirit appears as the inaugurating tongues of flame at the birth of the Church, and is everywhere associated with birth, as in the water poured in threefold blessing at baptism, when the child is pulled from the font as from the womb. That the Spirit should be characterized as maternal has nothing to do with accidents of grammar such as the fact that *Ruh* in Syriac and Aramaic is a feminine noun. No: the disposition of the Spirit is maternal as Immanent Cause, as that which fructifies from within, from its indwelling of the created world. *Spiritus Domini implevit orbem terrarum*, as the Psalmist says. But if the Spirit is the 'whereby' of the Son's generation in eternity and in time, Mary is the visible 'whereby' of the Son's temporal generation, and in deputizing for the Spirit, as it were, Mary bears

witness to the Spirit's generative power in herself, for it is by the power of the Spirit that she conceives. So one might say that the Spirit is the power of bringing–to–birth, and the visibility of the Spirit, Mary, the pure state of motherhood.

16. Despite the reservations of Aquinas, Pope John Paul II, in his Encyclical, *Mulieris Dignitatem*, uses obstetric imagery in speaking of God's engendering power. He speaks of 'the womb of God' bearing humanity, a mode of speech which goes back to *The Odes of Solomon* (circa 250 A.D.). In particular, the 19th Ode speaks of the Son issuing from 'the womb of his Father', but the maternal element thus introduced into the Father's personality is represented by the maternal Holy Spirit who functions as 'the womb of the Father' which gives birth to the Son. Since 'mankind was created originally as a kind of double image – as the image of the Son who is the image of the Father, but also as the image of the Son who is the child of Mary',[12] the Holy Spirit mediates between God the Father and Mary, as Jesus Christ is both Son of God and Son of Mary. The author of the 19th Ode emphasizes, however, the fact that Mary has no male consort in this birth–process, just as the Father had no female consort in the begetting of his Son.[13] And this, I think, is the point of the restriction placed by Aquinas on 'generation': he wants to preserve the absolute creativity of God as Pure Act from reliance on any mediating instrumentality. Thus the double birth of the Son – in eternity and in time – testifies to God's absolute creativity in respect of these two dimensions. For, in the former case, the eternal birth, God the Father generates God the Son through the Holy Spirit without the mediation of a heavenly Mother, and in the latter case, the temporal birth, God the Holy Spirit generates the incarnate Son, through the Virgin Mary, without the mediation of an earthly father – i.e. by power of parthenogenesis. None the less, expressions like 'the womb of the Father' put language under a severe strain, and although they are meant metaphorically, there is no need to have recourse to such metaphorically hybrid expressions when the literal meaning of 'the womb of Mary' is enough. If, like Mary, we are seeking to understand what is meant by God's Love, then surely we can say that the maternal Love of the Spirit is responsive to the paternal Love of the Father without impugning the absolute creativity of either – i.e. without admitting a heavenly mother or an earthly father? And if we can, then Mary's responsiveness to the persuasions of the Spirit will, in reiterating the Spirit's responsiveness to the Father, be the responsiveness of Wisdom to Word, or Sophia to Logos. To say that Wisdom is made flesh in Mary, meaning thereby that it is naturally embodied in her, is simply to say that Mary's conception is immaculate, so that in her immaculate womanhood she

may bear the immaculate manhood of the Word-made-flesh in her. The expressions 'immaculate womanhood' and 'immaculate manhood' should not, however, be taken to mean 'pure femininity' and 'pure masculinity', if only because, in any given instance of gender-specificity, the unexemplified gender is not absent; it is, rather, internalised.

17. If the Spirit of the Father is the *same* Spirit as the Spirit of the Son, the Spirit who is the same for both must be different from either.[14] How, then, does the Spirit differ from the Father and the Son? In being the Source of Maternity – i.e. the maternal co–efficient in generation, eternal and temporal. Since the Three Persons do not differ from one another in being God, but in the way each is God with respect to the other two, the way in which the Holy Spirit is God with respect to the Father and the Son will lie in its dispositional difference, in its being maternal. But if a 'maternal co–efficient' is admitted, are we speaking about an attribute of the Father and the Son, or about an attribute of the Spirit who 'proceeds from the Father and the Son'? Let it be granted that God the Father cannot give what is not already in him: even so, the maternally generative power of the Spirit would be actualized precisely in *being given by* the Father, so that 'proceeding from' would amount to the same as 'given by'. And if the co-eternal Spirit gives back to the Father what has been given by the Father, and equally, if it gives back to the Son what has been given by the Son, this double donation of the Spirit follows from the nature of the godhead – i.e. from the mutual self–giving that is definitive of Love. To this it may be objected that the Spirit's incarnational role is paternal rather than maternal. But is this really so? The Church has never accorded to the Spirit the title 'Father of the incarnate Son', even though it is by 'the power of the Holy Spirit' that Mary conceives. There is no suggestion of invagination in the birth–process, but, on the contrary, of a power of parthenogenesis working *from within* the natural order. As Immanent Cause, the Holy Spirit fructifies from within to without, and not from without to within.

18. Having rejected subordinationism in its trinitarian theology, the Church might perhaps consider rejecting subordinationism in its incarnational theology: at least I make so bold as to suggest that it might consider doing so, and for the following reasons. If responsibility for the Fall is shared equally between male and female, Adam and Eve, should not responsibility for its reversal be shared equally between Jesus and Mary? If the Second Person, or Form of Filiality, constitutes God's Humanity, then God's Humanity is no more divided, by being shared equally between Jesus and Mary, than our humanity is divided by being shared equally between male and

female. And if God's Humanity is to be conformable with our humanity, must not incarnation take on the male–female duality of our humanity? Jesus dies for humanity, male and female alike, and the Body which Mary gave him, the Body that lets God be Jesus Christ, is the same Body as that which he gives *for* us on the Cross and *to* us in the Eucharist. (The relation of physical body (corporality) to mystical body (corporeality) is thus established.) And if the Spirit which Mary receives at the Annunciation is the same Spirit as that which Jesus gives on the completion of his earthly ministry, there will be between them a symbiosis of the Spirit, as it were, and between the physical body and the mystical body a natal bond which allows the Annunciation-experience of Mary to be shared by the Church at Pentecost. Mary will, therefore, be able, as Figure of the Church, to intercede for the humanity, male and female alike, on behalf of which her Son suffered and died.

19. Granted that there is a relation of reciprocity between the mutual indwelling of the godhead's Three Persons and the gender–differences made manifest in the godhead's imaging (or exteriorization) of itself in the creation of humankind as male and female, then the original complementarity between male and female, distorted though it has been into various forms of subjugation as a result of the Fall, must surely be exemplified by the Second Adam, Jesus, and the Second Eve, Mary? This typological parallelism (which works by affinity as well as by contrast) has its own logic, and if it has been suppressed because it seems to endanger the *Solus Christus* principle, this is to mistake its purpose, for what it does is to introduce a principle of complementarity which, by disallowing subordination, allows us to say 'Blessed be each in the other'. And this means that the mediatorship of Jesus Christ (as the visibility of God the Father) is conveyed to us through Mary (as the visibility of the Holy Spirit); it means that the Holy Spirit gives us Jesus Christ from God the Father through Mary, and that Jesus Christ gives us Mary as Figure of the Church, to be raised, as he is raised, to God the Father through the Holy Spirit. This is what *coinherence* means – a Christ whose very relatedness constitutes his divine-human identity.

20. If the humanity that includes both male and female can be represented equally by either, or if, conversely, either is fully representative of the humanity that includes both, then what is definitive of humanity is neither the one nor the other, but the relation of equality between them. And if this is true of our humanity, it is true, *a fortiori*, of God's Humanity brought into conformity with ours. And if God is Love, then what is definitive of God's Humanity is also definitive of God's Love – the reciprocity of giving and receiving, or mutual self-giving. If each is cherished infinitely by the other, or if

each is the other's Beloved, then *what* is cherished – the object of Love's limitless regard – is the personhood of each, and that personhood cannot be divorced from its gender-related disposition. But *how* is that personhood cherished? By mutual self-giving. So the Beloved is, in a sense, beyond gender – not, however, in the sense that it has no gender, but in the sense that it does not matter which gender it has. Where unitive Love is the model, there is, one might say, unity in respect of the *how* and difference in respect of the *what*. Although a reciprocal relation is by definition a relation of equality, the equality here in question is equality between different persons, with different sensibilities, different life–histories, different sets of spatio–temporal co–ordinates. In other words, the incarnational equation is a *differential* equation; for although Jesus and Mary are equally representative of humanity, their roles are not interchangeable. So we must move from considerations of equality to the differential dynamic appropriate to *persons*, and when we do, we find a rhythm of reciprocity between the engendering power of God and God's being engendered under the conditions of our humanity, a reciprocity, that is, between divine fatherhood and human motherhood, between God's gender-conferring power and the specific genders which it externalises. Without specific gender there would be no such reciprocity, and without such reciprocity there would be no distribution of God's Love, no dispensation of Redemption.

21. Dante's great invocation – *Virgine Madre, figlia del tuo Figlio* – implies that God the Son engenders the Heavenly Daughter who is his earthly Mother, that the Logos, the Creative Word, the Exemplary Cause, projects, in the eternal order, the Exemplary Effect which inheres in it. And if so, then the earthly Mother engenders in time the Son by whom she is engendered in eternity. Given the transworld identity of the historical Jesus and the heavenly Jesus (i.e. given that Jesus of Nazareth and the Risen Jesus are one and the same person) and given, likewise, the transworld identity of the historical Mary and the heavenly Mary, then Mary assumed into heaven will stand in the same relation to her Son as that in which he stands to God the Father – namely, the filial relation which, in her case, is that of daughterhood. Consider for a moment the transpositions involved: in one direction – in the trajectory running from God's immanence to God's transcendence – earthly daughterhood (Mary as the immaculately conceived daughter of Joachim and Anna) becomes heavenly daughterhood (Mary assumed into heaven as the Daughter of her Son), and in the other direction – in the trajectory running from God's transcendence to God's immanence – heavenly sonhood becomes earthly sonhood. The parallelism is exact. And note how at the centre, the point at which the two trajectories inter-

sect, Mary, the daughter of Joachim and Anna, becomes Mary, the Mother of Jesus, and, since Jesus is the Word-made-flesh, the creatrix in time of him from whom she has her being in eternity. This is the heart of the mystery.

22. That the filial relation of daughterhood is implied by the Second Person's being the Form of Filiality follows from the logical properties of what it is to be a 'Form'. Thus, to say that the Second Person is the 'Form' of Filiality is to say that the Second Person is an instance of the propositional function 'x is f' being true for that value of x which is A.[15] That is to say, there is at least one value of x for which that propositional function is true. But there are in fact two values, for the simple reason that 'Filiality' takes two values, *Filius* and *Filia*, Son and Daughter. *The Form of* Filiality is, then, to be distinguished from the forms *in which* filiality is exemplified, and these forms will be the individuations of the Second Person. Logical form is that which enables us to say whatever we do say: it is thus anterior to any particular use to which words may be put. And, as logical form shows itself in the capability of propositions to make sense (by being either true or false) so the Form of Filiality shows itself in the capability of God to be incarnate. Hence, if 'Form of Filiality' means 'Incarnatability', the forms in which it is instantiated will be incarnate. And since 'Filiality' takes two values, the mode of incarnation will be different for each. In the case of divine sonhood it will, as already explained, take the form of a determinate event, and in the case of human daughterhood, it will take the form of a preparatory process leading up to that event.

23. But to return to the central relation. Mary assumed into heaven, we have said, stands in the same relation to her Son as that in which he stands to God the Father – namely, the filial relation which in her case is that of daughterhood. That is to say, the temporal Mother–Son relation is between the same two persons who are related eternally as Father and Daughter, Mary being both Mother and Daughter of Jesus, and Jesus being both Father and Son of Mary. Thus the temporal Mother-Son relation is convertible to the Father-Daughter relation, so that one might say that the Mother-Son relation is to the Father-Daughter relation as the temporal is to the eternal. But lest I should give the impression that there is an irreducible eternal-temporal, heavenly-earthly, dualism at work, I want to stress that we are dealing here, not with *two* relations, but with one relation of reciprocal love between two persons, Mary and Jesus – one relation which is such that time and eternity, earth and heaven, interpenetrate, for it is precisely such interpenetration that incarnation accomplishes. We have two terms and the reciprocal relation of Love between them. This relation of Love expresses the divine

nature. But the divine nature is not another term: it vanishes, so to speak, into the persons between whom the relation holds. The Love which is God gives both the meaning and the means, for what the convertible relation shows is Love as triune – as paternal-filial-maternal – both *ad intra*, in the interior life of the Trinity, and *ad extra* in the life–histories of Jesus and Mary.

24. We should speak, then, not of the *conjunction* of the eternal and the temporal in the union of incarnation, but of their *coinherence* – i.e. of the eternal-in-the-temporal and of the temporal-in-the-eternal. But for the eternal to be contained in the temporal, for the Logos, or Exemplary Cause, to be contained in the Exemplary Effect (e.g. for that period of interior growth in the womb of Mary which precedes the birth),[16] the temporal must be pre–contained in the eternal, the Exemplary Effect in the Exemplary Cause. Given that what is enfolded eternally is unfolded temporally, and that what is unfolded temporally is enfolded eternally, the relation of the eternal to the temporal will be that of the integral to the differential: i.e. eternity will be the integral of which time is the differential. [17]

25. When Mary assumed into heaven is said to stand in the same relation to her Son as that in which he stands to God the Father, the proportionality invoked should prevent any misunderstanding about the paternity of the Son. What the proportionality implies is that Mary is Daughter in relation to her Son: that is to say, 'Son' is convertible to 'Father' in respect of Mary's filial dependence on the Creative Word who is God the Son. But 'Son' is not convertible to 'Father' in respect of the filial dependence of Jesus on God the Father. Thus to attribute fatherhood to the Son does not imply that the Son is his own Father: it implies, rather, that the Logos, or Exemplary Cause, projects in eternity, or engenders, the Exemplary Effect by means of which the Father's Creative Word is made flesh. Or consider the relationships involved like this: the earthly motherhood of Mary is the visible sign of her heavenly daughterhood, and the earthly sonhood of Jesus is the visible sign of his heavenly fatherhood. Not that Jesus is his own father, but that the God who engenders is the same God as the God who is engendered – the same God as to nature, but not the same person. If this were not so, the filial dependence of the incarnate Son on his heavenly Father would be removed, and with it the dimension of transcendence. Indeed, the very possibility of such a misunderstanding raises a further consideration – the relation of potential fatherhood to actual sonhood, and of potential motherhood to actual daughterhood. As Eckhart says, 'We find filiation in potential fatherhood' and 'since a thing which comes out must first have been in',[18] the generation of the Son actualises God's fatherhood. But if God's fatherhood is actualised in the

begetting of the Son, the Son's fatherhood will be actualised in the Son's begetting – not his divine image, but his divine complement – for, if sonhood is potential fatherhood it must, in the divine case, be actual fatherhood, since there is no potentiality in God. Moreover, if the Son is paternally generative, the Daughter is maternally generative, for the same reason. In short, the fatherhood of the Son and the motherhood of the Daughter are implications of what is meant by saying that God is Pure Act.

26. When we say that the God who engenders is the same God as the God who is engendered, we distinguish the God who Begets from the God who is Begotten by adding the qualification, 'the same God as to nature, but not the same Person.' If, however, we say, not of the godhead, but of the Word-made-flesh, that 'the Vivifier is the Vivified', [19] then one and the same *person* is the subject of both predicates. And if it be granted that Jesus and Mary are individuations of the Second Person, and, as such, distinct *persons* who, nevertheless, share the same divine-human nature, as exemplars of God's Humanity, then the Vivifier-Vivified equation, as applied to both, would mean that the eternal vivifier is the temporally vivified (in the case of Jesus) and that the temporal vivifier is the eternally vivified (in the case of Mary). Thus the equation applies to Jesus *because* it also applies to Mary. In short, Jesus and Mary are mutually generative, given that incarnation is a transaction between the eternal temporalised in Jesus, and the temporal eternalised in Mary.

Conclusion

27. The convertible relation, whereby the Father-Daughter relation is seen as the inverse of the Mother-Son relation, has Love as its ligature – the Love of the engenderer for the engendered and of the engendered for the engenderer. What the convertible relation shows is the divine nature as coinherently paternal-filial-maternal: it encodes, as it were, what divine creativity presupposes – viz. the mutual indwelling of the Three Persons. If we take 'engendering' to mean both 'begetting' and 'bringing forth', then, as Mother, Mary will be the visibility of the Third Person's power of 'bringing forth', just as her son is the visibility of the First Person's power of 'begetting'. Thus, if the Second Person is both engendering and engendered – i.e. paternally generative as Son and filially generated as Daughter – its individuations are likewise both engendering and engendered, since Mary is maternally generative in the temporal order of the Son by whom she is herself engendered in the eternal order.

28. Since there is no subordination in the Trinity, it follows that if the convertible relation exhibits the paternal–filial–maternal dispositions of the godhead, then neither of the terms between which the convertible relation holds can be subordinate to the other.

Hence, parity of Persons in the Trinity entails the incarnational parity of its exponents. Furthermore, if we can say that Incarnation is the self-externalisation of the godhead, its paternal-filial-maternal dispositions will be externalised in the gender–specific individuations of the Second Person. That is to say, the mutual internality of the Three Persons will be externalised in the paternal-filial-maternal relations that hold between Mary as Mother-Daughter and Jesus as Father–Son. And such mutual internality will be co-intensive with their mutual externality as different persons. On the horizontal-temporal plane they have different life-histories, different time-tracks, but at every point on the horizontal plane one may posit an eternal-vertical axis which lets the daughter of Joachim and Anna be the Daughter of her Son, and the carpenter of Nazareth, the Son of Mary, be her progenitor as the Creative Word of God. The dynamic of divine Love will, then, be expressed in a rhythm of reciprocity between One Person in two natures and two persons in one nature – i.e. between the Second Person, the subject of God's Humanity, and two persons, its individuations, whose complementarity exhibits the nature of that Humanity. On this construal, the two natures ascribed by the Council of Chalcedon to the One Person of Jesus Christ would be *trans*cribed to the Second Person, and they would be so transcribed – (a) because in the Second Person the Exemplary Effect inheres in the Exemplary Cause, the temporal in the eternal, the human in the divine, and (b) because this prior configuration enables its incarnational reverse – namely, that in which the Exemplary Cause inheres in the Exemplary Effect, the eternal in the temporal, the divine in the human. Thus the filial dependence of the Daughter on the Father (as to eternal generation) is matched by the filial dependence of the Son on the Mother (as to temporal generation).

29. The Second Person is enclosed, as it were, by the First Person and the Third, and it is exactly designated by Coleridge's term 'Logosophia', a term which transparently signifies the union of Logos and Sophia, Word and Wisdom, Meaning and Understanding. The Second Person is, then, the *locus* of unitive Love, and the *transitus* from unitive Love to redemptive Love is effected by the Creative Word of the Father, God the Son; and it is effected (to repeat what has already been said) by the Son's being paternally generative, in the eternal order, of the Daughter by whom he is maternally generated in the temporal order. So what empowers incarnation is the Love between them, encircled, as that Love is, by the Love of God the Father for God the Son, in God the Holy Spirit.

30. It has been said that at the heart of every human love-relationship there is always a child waiting to be born. But at the heart of God's love-relationship with his handmaid – the created

world perfected in Mary – there is no waiting, except on the side of the creature; for *there*, in God's interior space, as it were, Love's issue is not the temporal *result* of union but its eternal *condition*. Declarations to the effect that 'God becomes as we are that we may become as God is'[20] attribute a redemptive purpose to God, but if what is made possible temporally by the fulfilment of that purpose, is already accomplished eternally, then *theosis* is not only the result, it is also the precondition of Incarnation. And that precondition is met by the Heavenly Daughter who is given the name of Mary and the role of God Incarnate's earthly Mother, for her occupancy of 'the metaphysical space' reserved for Sophia means that heaven and earth, eternity and time, divinity and humanity, are already one in the Second Person, and therefore in the mutual indwelling of the Three Persons.

31. What holds for the precondition of Incarnation holds equally for its result – the Resurrection of Jesus and the Assumption of Mary into Heaven. The seventeenth century visionary, the Spanish nun, Mary of Agreda, expresses the relation between these mysteries thus: 'the body of the glorified Lord encompassed and enclosed into itself the glorified body of his mother, and Mary was God with Jesus.'[21] Mary's Assumption is here the paradigm of that *theosis* which is promised to the Church. Note, however, that Mary is not said to be 'God', *simpliciter*, but, as a consequence of incarnation, to be 'God with Jesus' – an all–important qualification which supports the contention that God's individuated Humanity embraces Jesus *and* Mary. As to there being a precondition of incarnation, what could that be but the Trinity itself? Invoking a 'precondition' amounts to saying that *theosis* begins, where everything else begins, in the Trinity itself, and there is surely nothing exceptionable in that? As the mirrored reflection of the sun is, in the sun, sun, so 'the soul's reflection is, in God, God', wrote Eckhart, but he went on to say, '*There*, where God's utterance is God, God is not the creature, the creature is God'. [22] And the creature is, in God, God, because God is, in the creature, God.

32. By concentrating on the convertible relation, I hope to have brought into sharper focus the more generally problematic relation of creator to creature. To the objection that this exercise in revisionary theology lacks scriptural warrant, I can only reply that it is the function of theology to address the more general questions raised by scripture, rather than to support its reflections by appealing to particular texts at every point. Chief among the questions raised is the relation of God-as-engendering (Creator) to God-as-engendered (Incarnate), and it is one that has occupied Christian theology from the earliest times to the present day. In the *De Incar-*

natione, Athanasius puts the paradox thus: 'He formed his own body from the Virgin; and it is no small proof of his godhead, since he who made *that* was the Maker of all else.'[23] What I have proposed is in no sense a resolution of this paradox: it is, rather, an attempt to draw out some of its inexhaustible implications. If we conduct the thought–experiment of supposing that the First Person is Mother and the Second Person incarnate as Daughter, then, as Charles Davis has argued, our conceptualization of the Trinity will be unaffected. From this thought-experiment he derives the conclusion that neither fatherhood nor sonhood is essential to our conceptualization of the Trinity, since they could be replaced by motherhood and daughterhood without modification to its structure. Conducting a similar thought-experiment, I reach the opposite conclusion – not that neither is essential, but that both fatherhood-sonhood and motherhood-daughterhood are essential. By this I mean that both the Father-Son model and the Mother-Daughter model are equally true to the actuality of divine Love.

33. So, to recapitulate: the internal relations of the godhead are relations of coinherence holding between three subjects of paternal-filial-maternal dispositions. These three subjects, or Persons, exist only in relation to one another – as three focuses of one self-giving – and for them to be coinherent is for each to be articulated through the other two. Therefore, since the Second Person is articulated through the First Person and the Third (so that its individuations are their visible exponents), the originative paternal Love of the First Person and the responsive maternal Love of the Third Person transpire through the convertible relation that holds between *the Fatherhood of the Son* and *the Motherhood of the Daughter*, as these are realised in the persons of Jesus and Mary.

Notes

1. Dom Placid Kelley (C.F. Kelley),'Meister Eckhart's Doctrine of Divine Subjectivity', *Downside Review*, 1958, vol 76, 65–103; and *Meister Eckhart on Divine Knowledge*, (Yale, 1977), 167–172.

2. Wittgenstein, *Philosophical Investigations*, (Blackwell, 1953), II. iv. 178e.

3. Gerard Manley Hopkins, *Poems 1877*, No.7, 'God's Grandeur'.

4. Charles Davis,'The Maleness of Jesus', *The Tablet*, 18 Feb. 1989.

5. Henry Adams, *Mont Saint Michel and Chartres*, (CUP Library of America edition 1983), 1110f.

6. Dante, *Divina Commedia*, Paradiso, Canto XXXIII, line l.

7. Henry Corbin, *The Man of Light in Iranian Sufism*, Shambhala, 1978, 21f.

8. John Henry Newman, *Oxford Sermons*, (Longmans, Green, 1906), 66.

9. Wittgenstein, *On Certainty*, (Blackwell, 1969), 141, 142, 144e.

10. Austin Farrer, *The Revelation of St. John the Divine*, Commentary, (Oxford, 1964), 142f.

11. Aquinas, reference untraced.

12. Roberta C. Chesnut, *Three Monophysite Christologies*, (Oxford, 1976), 127ff.

13. Hans J.W. Drijvers, *East of Antioch*, (Variorum Reprints, 1984), 337– 355.

14. Anselm, *Trinity, Incarnation, and Redemption*: Theological Treatises edited Hopkins and Richardson, (Harper and Row, 1970), 'On the Procession of the Holy Spirit'. 84.

15. Michael Durrant, *The Logical Status of God*, (Macmillan, 1973), 54f and 63.

16. Charles Williams, *The Descent of the Dove*, (Longmans, 1939); reprinted Meridian Books, 1956), 234.

17. Evgheny Lampert, *The Divine Realm*, (Faber, 1944), 64.

18. *Meister Eckhart*, edited Ursula Fleming, (Fontana, 1988), 138f.

19. Ibn 'Arabī: Futūhāt IV, 367, as quoted in *The Passion of al-Hallaj* by Louis Massignon (trans Herbert Mason, Bollingen Series XCVIII, vol 2, Princeton, 1982), 396.

20. Irenaeus, *Adv Haer* 5, Pref; Athanasius, *De Inc.*, 54.

21. T.D. Kendrick, *Mary of Ágreda* (RKP, 1967) 89f.

22. C.F. Kelley, *Meister Eckhart on Divine Knowledge*, op cit, 104: references – Quint, 273, Pfeiffer, 180f.

23. Athanasius, *De Inc.*, 18.

Newman's mariology and his personal development

Sister Lutgart Govaert, STD
Roman Catholic, The Work, Littlemore, Oxford

If Mary is the Mother of God, Christ must be literally Emmanuel, God with us. And hence it was that, when time went on, and the bad spirits and false prophets grew stronger and bolder, and found a way into the Catholic body itself, then the Church, guided by God, could find no more effectual and sure way of expelling them than that of using this word *Deipara*, 'Mother of God', against them; and, on the other hand, when they came up again from the realms of darkness, and plotted the utter overthrow of Christian faith in the sixteenth century, then they could find no more certain expedient for their hateful purpose than that of reviling and blaspheming the prerogatives of Mary, for they knew full well that, if they could once get the world to dishonour the Mother, the dishonour of the Son would follow close. The Church and Satan agreed together in this, that Son and Mother went together; and the experience of three centuries has confirmed their testimony, for Catholics who have honoured the Mother, still worship the Son, while Protestants, who have now ceased to confess the Son, began then by scoffing at the Mother. [1]

From our knowledge of Newman's life we may gather that he did not always think about Mary in this way. We may ask: what happened from the days of his Anglican boyhood, when the ten-year-old John Henry drew a Rosary in his verse–book, until the convert spoke in such clear words about the necessity of Mary in the life of the Church? Answering this question we will trace the development of Newman's Mariology and the influence it had during his Anglican days.

When Newman was fifteen years of age, he 'fell under the influence of a definite Creed, and received...impressions of dogma, which, through God's mercy, have never been effaced or obscured.' [2]

Among the dogmas Newman then accepted were the doctrines of the Holy Trinity and of the Incarnation. Holy Scripture had been the source of his religious knowledge since his childhood,[3] and this scriptural principle was completed by the doctrine of Tradition. He learned from Dr Hawkins in the early 1820's that Holy Scripture 'was never intended to teach doctrine, but only to prove it. In order to learn doctrine we must have recourse to the formularies of the Church.'[4] At that time Tradition meant to Newman the Thirty–

Nine Articles of the Church of England, the Prayer Book and the Book of Homilies, as well as the Anglican Divines, and through them also the Fathers of the Church.

Newman's reflective faith in the Incarnation led him to assent to the doctrine of the Creed on Mary the Virgin and Mother of God. In 1832 Newman – then Fellow of Oriel College and Vicar of St Mary the Virgin in Oxford – preached a sermon on the reverence due to Our Lady. The Feast of the Annunciation inspired him. What he said however aroused the indignation of his congregation and he was accused of holding the doctrine of the Immaculate Conception.[5] Newman's offensive words read as follows:

> Who can estimate the holiness and perfection of her, who was chosen to be the Mother of Christ? If to him that hath, more is given, and holiness and divine favour go together (and this we are expressly told), what must have been the transcendent purity of her, whom the Creator Spirit condescended to overshadow with His miraculous presence? What must have been her gifts, who was chosen to be the only near earthly relative of the Son of God, the only one whom He was bound by nature to revere and look up to; the one appointed to train and educate Him, to instruct Him day by day, as He grew in wisdom and stature? This contemplation runs to a higher subject, did we dare to follow it; for what, think you, was the sanctified state of that human nature, of which God formed His sinless Son; knowing as we do, 'that which is born of the flesh is flesh', and 'none can bring a clean thing out of an unclean'?[6]

What Newman said is scriptural. Yet his congregation did not accept the consequences he indicated, because the revealed truths tended to be neglected among a great many Anglicans then. But Newman remained faithful to the great Christian doctrines which had gained such a hold on his mind since his first conversion in 1816. His sermons expounded them in a really balanced way and Newman became more and more influential during the 1830's, not only by what he said in the pulpit, but also by the strictness and holiness of his life which gave authority to his words.

In his sermons Newman insisted on the 'Catholic doctrine of the Incarnation of the Eternal Word'.[7] 'The Word was from the beginning, the Only–begotten Son of God'.[8] Christ is *True God*. With the same insistence he stresses His becoming *True* Man. It was not enough for Newman to explain that Christ was the eternal Word of God who became the Son of Man. Christ was one Person. That means that the Blessed Virgin, the Mother of Christ, is the Mother of this Person, who is truly God and man, the Word of God made man.

Newman sees in this doctrine of Our Lady as the Mother of God a safeguard for the doctrine of the Incarnation, as he preached in 1832:

> Nothing is so calculated to impress on our minds that Christ is really partaker of our nature, and in all respects man, save sin only, as to associate Him with the thought of her, by whose ministration He became our brother. [9]

Mary's title as Mother of God implies all her privileges, in the first place her virginity. Newman found in the Creed that 'Christ is conceived by the Holy Ghost born of the Virgin Mary' [10] and he had no doubt about it. It was even necessary and fitting because – as he said in 1834:

> when the Only–begotten Son stooped to take upon Him our nature, He had no fellowship with sin. It was impossible that He should. Therefore, since our nature was corrupt since Adam's fall, He did not come in the way of nature, He did not clothe Himself in that corrupt flesh which Adam's race inherits. He came by miracle, so as to take on Him our imperfection without having any share in our sinfulness. [11]

Already in 1828 Newman was reading the Fathers of the Church. Should we then be surprised to hear that they inspired him when he made an allusion here – as in his sermon on Our Lady of 1831 and 1832 – to the theme which would become fundamental for his Mariology: Mary as the Second Eve? Newman said:

> As in the beginning, woman was formed out of man by Almighty Power, so now, by a like mystery, but a reverse order, the new Adam was fashioned from the woman. [12]

This image of Mary as the Second Eve will constantly develop in Newman's Mariology and become the basic theme of his *Letter to Pusey*, Newman's only really mariological work, published in 1866. From this idea of Mary as the Second Eve he will derive all her privileges: her holiness, her dignity, her being the Immaculate Conception, her divine Motherhood, the power of her intercession...

In 1834 Newman had not yet reached this fulness. His doctrine is clear and will not change in these essential points: Mary is the Mother of God, the Ever Virgin, the Second Eve, the purest and holiest of all creatures, who was free from sin. These privileges enable her to fulfil her own role in the salvation of mankind, as Newman put it so meaningfully in 1832:

> And when sorrow came upon her afterwards, it was but that blessed participation of her Son's sacred sorrows, not the sorrows of those who suffer for their sins. [13]

It is an important idea in Newman and the secret of his holiness and his influence that faith should show itself in life and be developed as a consequence of being lived. In his Marian Sermon of 1831 Newman complained that this was not so in the Church of England – there was hardly any devotion to her:

> Yet alas, in these latter times, it cannot be denied, we have in great measure forgotten to fulfil her meek anticipation of her own praise (From henceforth all generations shall call me blessed) ... Why should we not devoutly pay that honour which is promised as the Virgin's reward? Why not honour Our Lord in our respectful mention of His Mother? Why, because some Christians exceed in their devotion, become irreverent? Yet so it is. We do not think of St Mary as we ought. [14]

These last words lead us to ask whether Newman himself was devoted to Mary and how he saw this. Devotion is a consequence of faith and as faith in Christ was the driving centre of his life, so his faith in Mary brought him to a true devotion which he at once set out to practise in the Anglican Church.

The important question is: how did the Anglican Newman express this devotion? Newman advocated that reverence for Our Lady had to be expressed within certain limits. In 1831 he stated that we are safe in following Christ's example:

> When we estimate the reverence which her Son showed her, then we may know how fitly to honour her memory. [15]

And one year later he laid down a similar principle, based on the fact that Scripture does not say much about her:

> Had the Blessed Virgin Mary been more fully disclosed to us in the heavenly beauty and sweetness of the spirit within her, true, she would have been honoured, her gifts would have been clearly seen; but, at the same time, the Giver would have been somewhat less contemplated ... She would have been seemingly introduced for her sake, not for His sake. [16]

In these last words the position of the Anglican Newman with regard to devotion is summarized. He accepted all the great doctrines on Our Lady and had a personal devotion to her, remembering her for Christ's sake. At the same time he was faithful to the teaching of the Church of England not to give undue worship to Our Lady and the saints at the cost of the Creator, as was believed to happen in the Church of Rome. In the *Apologia pro Vita Sua* we read:

> The more I grew in devotion both to the Saints and to Our Lady, the more impatient was I at the Roman practices, as if those glorious creations of God must be gravely shocked, if pain could be theirs, at the undue veneration of which they were the objects. [17]

Newman's attitude concerning devotion was dictated by several doctrines he found in the Anglican Church, a few of them allowing some form of devotion, others restricting it. Let us have a closer look at some of them. The Oxford Movement, started in 1833, aimed at the revival of doctrines maintained by the great Anglican divines of the seventeenth century. Among these doctrines one of the most important was the doctrine of the visible Church, which for Newman did not exist without a strong link to the supernatural reality of the invisible Church. This doctrine embraces the sacramental principle and the article of the 'Communion of Saints'. Preaching about this latter doctrine in 1837 Newman was convinced that there is a relation between the Church on earth and the saints in heaven, that the saints are not useless to the visible Church. His question was: What can they do for us? The Anglican divines do not give a clear answer. One of them, Pearson, in his *Exposition of the Creed* mentioned 'desires and supplications on their side'. Newman found numerous examples of intercessory prayer in Holy Scripture. Though the legitimacy of intercession was not generally accepted in the Anglican Church, Newman felt safe. Looking closer at the Thirty–Nine Articles of his Church, he discovered that the Invocation of Saints is condemned as dangerous only because it may easily lead to undue worship of creatures at the cost of the Creator. But nothing is said about intercession. Consequently Newman distinguishes between Invocation, which he rejected, and Intercession, which he accepted. He rejected invocation because the Anglican Church teaches that the practice is not primitive, but an addition, because he was told by his Church to pray to God only and because he thought that the saints act as a body and not individually. This was Newman's view about 1837. Already in 1836 Newman had started to read regularly the offices of the Roman Breviary. There was not so much in them that seemed corrupt; he only hesitated to use the antiphons of the Blessed Virgin, ancient and simple as they were, and devoted as he was to her. It was not – as we have already seen – the Anglican usage to address her directly, and he felt it would be disloyal to do so without authority.[18] The question of invocation remained on Newman's mind.

There are still other principles which caused Newman to condemn the Roman devotion to Our Lady and the Saints. His great argument against Rome was, that it had added to the primitive teaching of the church. Newman distinguished between an Episcopal tradition and a Prophetical tradition. The episcopal tradition hands all the doctrines down to us from the Apostles through the Bishops. This tradition teaches the faithful the Creed, all the truths they really need for their salvation. The prophetical tradition is a more popular form of tradition, which may lead to corruption, if the Church is not careful to watch it continually. Newman considers this tradition partly to be a legitimate and therefore acceptable interpretation of the Creed, partly to be an innovation. And these innovations are to be condemned according to the Thirty–Nine Articles of the Anglican Church, which teach that Holy Scripture contains all that is needed for salvation. Following the Articles and the divines, especially Bishop Bull, one of the divines of the 17th Century, Newman accepted at this time also the mere verbal development of the doctrine contained in Holy Scripture: this means that the words may change but nothing can be added to the content and no real growth or development is possible. Thus Newman condemned the Roman practices saying:

> Surely, we have more reasons for thinking that her doctrines concerning Images and Saints are false, than her decision that they are Apostolical is true. [19]

This was Newman's view until the end of 1842. In the beginning of 1841 Newman tried to show in Tract 90 that the Catholic views of the Oxford Movement could be reconciled with subscription to the Thirty–Nine Articles of the Church of England, and that, although certain Roman doctrines were reprobated in the Articles, they were mainly directed against the actual popular belief and usages of Roman Catholics, which constituted an addition to the teaching of the Church. In Tract 90 Newman approved of various forms of invocation: for instance as addressed to invisible beings, since this is done daily in the Liturgy and the Psalms. Newman found an argument in Holy Scripture: the seven spirits before God's throne send us grace and peace and it is only natural that we should make our wishes known to them. Nor do the Homilies – which are of authority in the Anglican Church – reject invocation to beings who cannot hear, as long as we do not pray for anything definite, and when using these prayers as interjections.[20] While Newman gave a Catholic interpretation of the Thirty–Nine Articles in Tract 90 he maintained that the practical Roman teaching on Purgatory, Indulgences, the honours paid to images and relics, the invocation of saints and the Mass could not be reconciled with primitive doctrine. This Tract was intended to be a remedy, but it was condemned.

But Tract 90 had also a happy consequence for Newman. Dr Russell, a young Maynooth Professor, read it and wrote to Newman to remonstrate against the misinterpretations of Catholic doctrine, especially Transubstantiation, contained in it. Newman answered by making his distinction between the Roman doctrine – which he accepted in many points – and the 'traditionary system' which he considered to be a corruption. He complained especially about the excesses in the Roman devotion to Our Lady. Dr Russell then recommended that he study Catholic devotional writings about Our Lady in order to see whether or not they forget the honour due to God, and to Him alone. In addition, he sent Newman a volume of St Alfonsus' Sermons. Newman already knew quotations from them, but reading the whole, he did not find in them the idolatry he had expected and he was even more astonished to find that in one of the Sermons on Our Lady there were omissions. This fact made it clear to Newman that some devotional manifestations may be suitable for Catholics in Italy, but not therefore necessarily for Catholics in England. After having read St Alfonsus' Sermons Newman had all the elements for the distinction that will be so helpful in his Catholic days when corresponding with Anglicans and converts; the distinction between doctrine and devotion, which he will make the first point of his *Letter to Pusey*. Doctrine is always and everywhere the same; devotion is the personal expression of faith and may vary according to person, to time, to place. He began to understand that devotion to the saints is not an interference with the honour due to God, as he wrote in the *Apologia*:

> The devotions then to Angels and Saints as little interfered with the incommunicable glory of the Eternal, as the love which we bear our friends and relations, our tender human sympathies, are inconsistent with that supreme homage to the heart of the Unseen which really does but sanctify and exalt, not jealously destroy, what is of earth. [21]

He was quite astonished to find how little there was to which he could object in the cheap books of devotion sent to him by Dr Russell. Nevertheless, Newman had not yet quite overcome his difficulty on the score of the devotion paid to the Saints. It took him until 1844 before he got over it.

It was at this time, from the end of 1842 to 1844, that Newman applied his mind to the principle of development of doctrine in the Christian Church. He was interested in the question whether a true development, a true growth, is possible and how to discern it from an innovation and corruption. This question was of crucial importance, since Newman still suspected the Church of Rome of having added new doctrines and practices to the original Creed.

In the *Apologia* Newman suggested that there is a link between his new insight in Marian doctrine and devotion in the Roman Church and his study of the development of doctrine. He wrote:

> The idea of the Blessed Virgin was as it were *magnified* in the Church of Rome, as time went on, – but so were all the Christian

ideas; as that of the Blessed Eucharist. The whole scene of pale, faint, distant Apostolic Christianity is seen in Rome, as through a telescope or magnifier. The harmony of the whole, however, is of course what it was. [22]

Newman made the development in religious doctrine the subject of his last University Sermon, preached on February 2nd, the feast of the Purification, 1843. He chose St Mary as our example in both *receiving* Divine Truth and in *developing* it.

She does not think it enough to accept, she dwells upon it; not enough to possess, she uses it; not enough to assent, she develops it; not enough to submit the Reason, she reasons upon it; not indeed reasoning first, and believing afterwards, with Zacharias, yet first believing without reasoning, next from love and reverence reasoning after believing. And thus she symbolizes to us, not only the faith of the unlearned, but of the doctors of the Church also, who have to investigate, and weigh, and define, as well as profess the Gospel; to draw the line between truth and heresy; to anticipate or remedy the various aberrations of wrong reason; to combat pride and recklessness with their own arms; and thus to triumph over the sophist and the innovator. (*US 15:* 313–4)

In these same years Newman translated some writings by St Athanasius. He did not find there anything explicitly about Our Lady, but he discovered the theological principle of devotion to the saints, as he explained it in his *Essay on the Development of Christian Doctrine*, a work he wrote in 1845 and which he left unfinished on being received into the Roman Catholic Church. Newman realized that as a consequence of the Incarnation and Redemption, those who believe in Christ are given power to become sons of God in Him (Jn 1:12), and he concluded from this that

those who are formally recognized as God's accepted sons in Christ, are fit objects of worship on account of Him who is in them; a doctrine which both interprets and accounts for the invocation of Saints, the cultus of relics, and the religious veneration in which even the living have sometimes been held, who, being saintly, were distinguished by miraculous gifts. Worship then is the necessary correlative of glory; and in the same sense in which created natures can share in the Creator's incommunicable glory, are they also allowed a share of that worship which is His property alone. [23]

Newman also discovered how the image of Our Lady became ever clearer in the first centuries of the Church. After the condemnation of the Arians it was shown that to exalt a creature was no recognition of its divinity. [24]

because as Newman said,

> Arius or Asterius did all but confess that Christ was the Almighty; they said much more than St Bernard or St Alphonso have since said of the Blessed Mary; yet they left Him a creature and were found wanting.[25]

It fascinated Newman to realize that, when Arianism was condemned, the high place which the Arians had ascribed to Christ, that is the place of the most exalted creature – was left open. This was the place of Mary, the Mother of God.[26] The formal ecclesiastical decision about her dignity was only given in the fifth Century, when the Council of Ephesus defined her to be the Theotokos, the Mother of God. As such she had always been present in the spontaneous or traditional feeling of Christians. The definition of her title by the teaching authority of the Church at that particular moment served a purpose, as Newman said:

> In order to honour Christ, in order to defend the true doctrine of the Incarnation, in order to secure a right faith in the manhood of the Eternal Son.[27]

Thus Newman had overcome all difficulties he once had with regard to the Roman devotion to Our Lady and he recognized in her the role in which he will honour her so much, that is, the 'Seat of Wisdom': the safeguard of true faith in Christ, our model for the reception of faith and its development in the soul.[28] The Catholic Newman will keep Our Lady before the eyes of the faithful as an example, as a guide on their way to Christ. He preached:

> Her glories are not only for the sake of her Son, they are for our sakes also. Let us copy her faith, who received God's message by the angel without a doubt; her patience, who endured St Joseph's surprise without a word; her obedience, who went up to Bethlehem in the winter and bore Our Lord in a stable; her meditative spirit, who pondered in her heart what she saw and heard about Him; her fortitude, whose heart the sword went through; her self–surrender, who gave Him up during His ministry and consented to His death.[29]

After having thus sketched Newman's changing and developing views concerning devotion to Our Lady, we can conclude with some thoughts on the place devotion to Our Lady held in his teaching.

Newman saw the relation of Marian devotion to adoration of Christ and of the work of Mary to that of Christ, as grounded on Mary's *Fiat* at the Annunciation, when she spoke her readiness to serve and her willingness for the working out of God's plan of salvation. Newman repeatedly defined this relation as service. He saw Mary's service as twofold: in the Catholic Church, Mary has shown herself not the rival, but the minister of her Son:

> She has protected Him, as in His infancy, so in the whole history of the Religion. [30]

The character of service in Mary's work had been clearly shown in the history of the Church. In 1849, Newman had proclaimed once again the fact of the gradual realisation of Mary's greatness, as he had already maintained in the *Essay on Development*, and in this light:

> When she and the Apostles had left this lower scene, and she was a Queen upon her Son's right hand, not even then did she ask of Him to publish her name to the ends of the world or to hold her up to the world's gaze, but she remained waiting for the time, when her own glory should be necessary for His. He indeed had been from the very first proclaimed by Holy Church, and enthroned in His temple, for He was God; ...but it was otherwise with Mary. It became her, as a creature, a mother and a woman, to stand aside and make way for the Creator, to minister to her Son, and to win her way into the world's homage by sweet and gentle persuasion. So when His name was dishonoured, then it was that she did Him service; when Emmanuel was denied, the Mother of God (as it were) came forward. [31]

This truth is not exemplified in history alone. Newman showed how it can be maintained not only from the written sources of the Church's Tradition; it is also conveyed by the daily life of the Church. Newman brought together some examples of the distinction made in the understanding of the faithful regarding Christ and Mary: the reverence shown by Catholics in their Churches flows from the real presence of Christ, not from the images of our Lady, crucifixes, and so on. The Mass too conveys 'the same lesson of the sovereignty of the Incarnate Son', the sacrifice ever renewed of Calvary where Mary truly withdraws into the background. So too is Holy Communion

> a solemn unequivocal act of faith in the Incarnate God, if any can be such; and the most gracious of admonitions, did we need one, of His sovereign and sole right to possess us. [32]

These quotations show that Newman always remained conscious of the proper place devotion to Our Lady has with regard to the adoration and honour due to her Son. This does in no way imply that his devotion to Mary lacked in quality and depth, as these concluding words of one of his sermons prove:

The Church gives us Jesus Christ for our food, and Mary for our nursing Mother ... Prove to the world that you are following no false teaching, vindicate the glory of your Mother Mary, whom the world blasphemes, in the very face of the world, by the simplicity of your own deportment, and the sanctity of your words and deeds. Go to her for the royal heart of innocence. She is the beautiful gift of God, which outshines the fascinations of a bad world, and which no one ever sought in sincerity and was disappointed. She is the personal type and representative image of that spiritual life and renovation in grace, 'without which no one shall see God'. [33]

Notes

1. Newman J.H., *Discourses Addressed to Mixed Congregations* (*Mix*) 348.
2. Newman J.H., *Apologia pro Vita Sua* (*Apo*) 4.
3. Ibid 1.
4. Ibid 9.
5. *Meditations and Devotions of the late Cardinal Newman* (*MD*) 79.
6. Newman J.H., *Parochial and Plain Sermons* (*PS*) II 131–132.
7. Ibid 32–3.
8. Ibid 30.
9. Ibid 136.
10. Ibid 31.
11. Ibid.
12. Ibid.
13. Ibid 137.
14. Govaert L., *Kardinal Newmans Mariologie und sein persönlicher Werdegang.* Salzburg 1975, 136.
15. Ibid 139.
16. *PPS* II 134.
17. *Apo* 53.
18. Cf Trevor M., *Newman. The Pillar of the Cloud* (New York 1962), 195.
19. Newman J.H., *Via Media* II 265.
20. Ibid 305.
21. *Apo* 196.
22. Ibid.
23. Newman J.H., *An Essay on the Development of Christian Doctrine* 142.
24. Ibid 144.

25. Ibid 143.
26. Ibid 143f.
27. Ibid 145.
28. Cf. Murray P., *Newman the Oratorian* (Dublin 1969), 79 n3.
29. *Mix* 374–5.
30. Newman J.H., *Certain Difficulties felt by Anglicans in Catholic Teaching* (*Diff*) II 93.
31. *Mix* 357.
32. Cf *Diff* II 93–96.
33. *Mix* 376.

Mary in the theology of Karl Barth

Paul S. Fiddes, M.A., DPhil.

Baptist, Principal, Regent's Park College, Oxford

In November, 1950, Pope Pius XII pronounced the Assumption of the Blessed Virgin Mary to be a dogma of the Church. A seat was reserved for Karl Barth in St Peter's for this solemn occasion, and although in the end he could not take up the place, he expressed his wish to be present. He wanted (he said), 'to be there for once when somebody makes an infallible statement.'[1]

This anecdote reveals a couple of significant things about the attitude of Karl Barth, as a very Protestant and Reformed theologian, to the whole scope of Mariology. In the first place, its ironic tone does not seem to promise well for ecumenical relations. Indeed, Barth believed that such veneration of Mary as was practised in the Roman Church was a hindrance to the ecumenical efforts he supported, and that it cast a shadow across the several deep friendships he enjoyed with Roman Catholic theologians. He remarked sadly a little later that 'the decisions made in 1950 have closed several doors, and in view of that we must keep our distance to begin with.'[2] But the incident also draws attention to the fact that Barth was always particularly interested in the subject of devotion to Mary. Admittedly, it was a kind of *negative* interest: he regarded Mariology as the central dogma of the Roman Catholic Church, 'in terms of which all [her] important positions are to be regarded and by which they stand or fall.'[3] Furthermore, beyond the question of the Roman Church, he saw the phenomenon of Mariology as a focus for mistaken thinking about the whole relationship of humankind to the grace of God revealed in Jesus Christ.

This wider anthropological theme is the one upon which I intend to concentrate here. In so doing, however, I want to suggest that Barth's thoughts about the place and honour of Mary may in fact reveal some ambiguities in his theology, some open ends in the tight weave and pattern of his system. The event of the faith and obedience of Mary, with her prayer 'let it be so to me', poses a challenge to Barth's theology as to all theologies. It is the test case which both brings out his best insights about the grace of God, but also exposes (I believe) some of his limitations.

The comment of Barth with which I began, passing though it be, points us to a basic feature of his objections to Mariology. His linking of the dogma of Mary with the claim of the Church to make infallible pronouncements makes clear that the issue for Barth is the limits and the capacities of human beings before God. So we notice that he certainly understands the nature of devotion to Mary which is expressed in the Catholic tradition (whether Roman or not). He is debating in the same arena; that is, he understands the issue to be in what sense Mary can be the prototype of *humanity*. When the title of 'Mother of believers' is given to Mary or the Church (and Barth sees the second as based on the first) the question is whether *human beings* are able to be mediators of divine grace. He firmly rejects any idea that Catholic veneration of Mary as 'Mother of God' imagines her to be a kind of goddess, or a fourth person within the Trinity. Here he makes a refreshing break from much former and crude Protestant polemic. As typical of the Catholic dogma of Mary, he quotes Thomas Aquinas that 'the mother of God is pure creature'.[4] In the Catholic tradition, he asserts, Mariology

> ... depends upon the fact that in spite of her infinite dignity, in spite of her incomparable privileges, and in spite, nay because of her cooperation in redemption, Mary ... belongs wholly to the creaturely, indeed to the earthly, human sphere. [5]

So Barth has rightly set out the boundaries for ecumenical discussion, identifying the crucial point from which all theologians can begin. We turn therefore to the question of Mary's special dignity as a human being, and Barth's answer to this will occupy the first major section of this paper.

1. Barth's view of the place of Mary in the history of salvation

Barth affirms the description of Mary as 'Mother of God', bearing the ancient title *Theotokos*.[6] This makes clear, explains Barth, that he who was born of Mary in time is the very same Son who was born eternally of the Father. So we are not to seek for revelation, for the 'Word of God', anywhere else than in the Son who was born of Mary. Throughout his theological work, when Barth refers to 'The Word of God' he does not mean that God has issued a message, or a set of propositions, or a list of commands, or even a sacred book. The Word of God in its primary sense is God's self-unveiling, nothing less than God himself coming to speak to us.[7] Thus Mary can indeed be called Mother of God, for she conceives and gives birth to Christ who *is* the Word of God, or 'the Person of God speaking'.

This means, in Barth's view, that the Virgin Mary represents humankind as receiver of the Word of God. She is 'full of grace' in the sense that she is a human being 'to whom the miracle of revelation happens'.[8] Barth's whole theological system rests upon the belief that man is not himself capable of receiving the word of God. There is no bridge from human experience in itself to the mystery of God, no natural link between human words and the divine word. There is, in a fallen human race, no capacity or disposition for God. Rather, God must take the total initiative in unveiling himself to us. He speaks to us and in so doing he makes us capable of hearing him. We cannot hear the Word, for we are in a state of rebellion, blocking our ears against him; but by the miracle of grace he makes us hear him. [9]

Above all in Christ God has spoken to us the word of justification; he has pronounced that we are 'in the right' with him. There is then no contribution that human beings can make to the act of salvation. Justification is solely an act of God in the cross and resurrection of Jesus; he has acted to put humankind in a right relationship with himself, and human beings are simply called upon to receive this gift. We are called to recognise the objective judgement that has already been passed by God upon all humankind in Christ. [10]

Mary, affirms Barth, was called like this in a definitive way. In her virginity she represents the inability of the human race to contribute anything to the coming of the Word of God which strikes at our existence and saves us. In her submissive word 'let it be so; behold the handmaid of the Lord' she shows a passive acknowledgement of what God alone can do. The virgin birth, Barth explains, is a sign of pure receptivity. In face of the creative act of God the whole human race is virgin, that is, unable for itself to make any point of connection to divine grace:

> ....in the birth without previous sexual union of man and woman
> (of which scripture speaks), man is involved in the form of
> Mary, but involved only in the form of *virgo Maria*, i.e. only
> in the form of non-willing, non-achieving, non-creative, non-
> sovereign man, only in the form of man who can merely receive,
> merely be ready, merely let something be done to and with
> himself. This human being, the *virgo*, becomes the possibility,
> becomes the mother of God's Son in the flesh. It is not, of
> course that she is this; but she becomes it. [11]

Virginity thus sums up the helplessness of human beings in the face of divine grace. Barth insists on a literal and historical virgin birth, but he does not think that the virginity of Mary contributes of itself to the saving event of incarnation. The manner of the birth does not make Jesus Christ what he is – truly God and truly man.[12] If the virgin birth actually constituted the being of Jesus, that would be a kind of divine marriage in which God could not be fully God. Nor does the manner of the birth cause the sinlessness of Jesus; here Barth objects to the tracing of sinlessness back to an immaculate conception of Mary. Rather, Jesus is the God-man, and he is free from sin, simply because of the free decision of God that the eternal Son should be identified with the man Jesus of Nazareth. However, the virgin birth of Jesus is essential for the gospel as a *sign* which

God gives in history of his new creative act. A birth through the normal sexual union of man and woman would not be a proper sign of incarnation.

This is not, according to Barth, because the human act of reproduction is the means of passing on original sin; sexual life is certainly sinful, but it shares this with all fallen human life. Rather, the event of sexual generation is unsuitable as a sign of incarnation because it is 'the work of willing, achieving, creative, sovereign man'.[13] The partners in human generation are highly active and creative, achieving something themselves. But only God achieves salvation; he is alone the Lord when he makes the cause of humankind his own. Moreover, Barth adds, there is something peculiarly suitable about the exclusion of the male from the virgin birth, and the singling out of the female of the species to be involved. Throughout history, of the human partners it is the male who appears to have played the more active part. Feminists will (at least partly) be pleased to note that Barth throws doubt on whether this is actually the case:

> God alone knows whether the history of humanity, nations and states, art, science, economics, has been and is so predominantly the history of males, the story of all the deeds and works of males, as it appears to be ... [14]

Yet this is the situation that is familiar to us, and so it is apt that the active (and aggressive?) male is removed from this most significant moment of all history. Let women, remarks Barth, who demand rehabilitation in the face of long male dominance take this as a sign of a limit on male pre-eminence. When God in his revelation and reconciliation 'makes room for himself among us, man and his sin are limited and judged,' and the more active the male, the more he falls under judgement.[15]

For Barth, the credal confession 'born of the Virgin Mary' makes clear that in this event of salvation 'no one is left to be God's fellow-worker'.[16] The male is removed entirely, and the virgin woman is present simply as the one 'upon whom and with whom God acts in his revelation'. Only a virgin birth can be the sign of incarnation, but the virgin birth does not contribute to incarnation. The reason in both cases is the same: man – represented by Mary – is simply the receiver of the Word. Now it should be clear what kind of veneration of Mary Barth is objecting to, and what he rejects as unacceptable Mariology. It is any view of Mary, and so any view of humankind in general, as co-worker with God in bringing about salvation (synergism). He sets out exactly what he rejects in these words:

> The 'Mother of God' of ... Marian dogma is quite simply the principle, type and essence of the human creature cooperating servant-like in its own redemption on the basis of prevenient

grace, and to that extent the principle, type and essence of the church.[17]

Barth is here rejecting the view that God first gave special grace to Mary, and that on the basis of such endowment she was inclined to cooperate with the Spirit of God. In such a case she would earn merit through her work of obedience. But the only glory can be God's, as the act of salvation is his alone. Barth says of Mary that 'she does not become the Mother of God through her own capacity; she acquires capacity by the act of the Son of God assuming flesh.' She may be called 'blessed' as the poor in the beatitudes are called 'blessed', in the sense that the Kingdom of God has come near to them in Jesus Christ. Barth here lays weight on the words of Elizabeth to Mary in Luke 1:45:

Blessed is she who believed; for there shall be a performance of those things which were told her from the Lord.

The blessedness, points out Barth, is in the performance by God, not a matter of inner virtue but a matter of our being lit up in a new way by the Lordship of God which has been revealed to us in Christ.[18]

So Barth recalls and opposes a cluster of images about Mary that are typical of Catholic devotion, and which link together motherhood, creativeness and unfallen nature. He points out that the motherhood of Mary is often envisaged as a desire for grace, a desire to conceive the Word. This motherhood is in turn attributed to the Church as giving birth to Christ in the sacraments. At the same time, motherhood is seen as a sharing in creation with God, and so a type of Mary is found in the figure of divine Wisdom. The female figure of Wisdom is depicted in scripture as active in creating the world on God's behalf, and though the early Fathers tended to identify this fruitful Wisdom with the Logos (Christ), Mariology has associated her with Mary. Further, such creativity is ascribed in the book of Genesis to unfallen man, and so Barth discerns a composite figure of Mary-Mother-Wisdom-Creatress in whom the image of God is restored by grace to its unfallen glory before the birth of Jesus.[19]

A poem by the Jesuit priest Gerard Manley Hopkins brings together all these images, in the way that Barth precisely rejects. In 'The May Magnificat' Hopkins asks why May should be chosen as Mary's special month in the liturgical Calendar:

Ask of her, the mighty mother:
Her reply puts this other
' Question: What is Spring?-
Growth in everything ...

All things rising, all things sizing
Mary sees, sympathising
   With that world of good,
   Nature's motherhood ...

This ecstasy all through mothering earth
Tells Mary her mirth till Christ's birth
   To remember and exultation
   In God who was her salvation. [20]

Hopkins finally makes clear that salvation is from God, but he does allow Mary a part in creating the new life God gives. Barth's own view of Mary fits in, as we have seen, with his view of the human condition. There is no openess to the Word of God already existing in fallen man. The Word creates the openness when it comes to us, so that *everything* in salvation is God's work.[21] If we were to think of Mary as inclined to receive the Word of God through the grace already existing within her, we would have to say this in some degree of all human beings.

2. Mary's response and human response to God

So far it may be felt that my opening prediction was all too true – Barth's understanding of the place and honour of Mary hardly seems likely to advance ecumenism in this area. However, I shall now venture to suggest that there are certain aspects of Barth's own thought that might encourage us to find rather more of a salvific co-working between God and humankind in Mary's response to God – 'let it be to me according to your word' – than Barth intends to allow. This in turn would require us to say rather more about the particular blessedness and honour of Mary than Barth does.

In the first place, we ought to be aware that Barth's emphasis upon the passivity of humankind before God stems from a pressing need to deal with the social and political problems of his time. He is, as we have seen, anxious to break any bridge between natural human existence and knowing God. He insists that the image of God in man is now defaced (though not obliterated), and so gives man no point of contact with God until the Word of God is spoken to re-create it. He also rejects the doctrine of an *analogia entis*, a natural correspondence of being between God and man, between Creator and creature, Lord and servant. God must himself *make* man correspond with him through the grace of redemption.[22] But we must not miss Barth's motivation for taking what seems to be a very dogmatic view of the utter sovereignty of God and the impossibility of a natural theology. He is afraid that if we try to work our way from human experience and human reason to God we shall create a God in our own image, and he sees that this has profound implications for human justice and freedom as well as for right theology.

When the leading German Protestant theologians signed a manifesto supporting the Kaiser's war plans of 1914, Barth began to develop a theology of the word of God spoken from beyond us, and not under the control of human ambitions. Later, when the so-called 'German Christian' Churches celebrated Hitler and his policies as a revelation of divine purpose for the German nation, Barth insisted that there could be no other mediator of divine grace than Jesus Christ. Humankind must simply receive the divine Word that overturns human existence. With the need sharply to confront such political pretensions, it is hardly surprising that Barth developed an extreme view of man's natural incapacity to respond to God, with a consequent suspicion of any devotion to Mary as the handmaid of the Lord who was able of her own accord to say 'yes'. The failure of the Churches during that period also helps to account for his suspicion of the Church's claim to share the motherhood of believers ascribed to Mary.

Since, however, we are not facing the same dangers as Barth was in his time, we might be able to accept his insights into the Lordship and grace of God, while allowing more place to the response of human beings and especially of Mary. With welcome clarity Barth stresses the objective act of God in salvation, to which we can add nothing as helpless and sinful creatures. He rightly understands justification to be God's judgement of human life, declaring us to be in the right with him as a sheer gift. He has got to the heart of human relationship with God when he insists that we can only know God because God reveals himself to us. As sinful and finite beings, we cannot unveil God; he must take the initiative and speak his word to us. In all this God acts objectively for us. But we must then ask – what of the subjective human appropriation of God's saving acts, the response of faith? Barth describes the human response as pure 're-ceptivity', a simple 'confirmation'[23] of what God has completed in Christ. We decide only on the basis of God's decision for us.[24] Nevertheless, is not the 'yes and amen' to God's verdict still highly *active*? Even passive reception is getting oneself involved in what God is doing.[25]

The response of faith seems to be a kind of cooperation with God that belongs somewhere in the arena of salvation, even if it is not a co-working in the reconciling act. Indeed, in a later section of his *Church Dogmatics* dealing with faith, Barth admits that faith must have a 'creative' character,[26] since the result of faith is new birth and a change of life in the believer. This becomes clear when we realise that what we call 'justification' and 'sanctification' are only two dimensions of the same event. Barth himself insists that sanctification (being made right) does not merely follow justification (being called right) as a later stage.[27] At the very same time as God announces that we are in the right with him he also begins to create us anew,[28] and human faith has a part in that creation.

This seems to leave a place for human cooperation with the work of salvation, at least in the subjective area of a transformed life. But of course Barth insists that this creativity of faith still owes everything to God; it is brought into being by the Holy Spirit at work within us, and 'we can only repeat this Yes of His'.[29] Put another way, faith 'lives from its object', who is Christ. [30]

The Word of God cannot, we might say, be conceived impersonally like a radio wave because there is no receiving apparatus already there, waiting to receive it. There is nothing in us which makes us 'capable of receiving the Word'. However, Barth here is wrestling with a problem. He wants to affirm that the act of faith is still a genuinely *human* one, with real responsibility.[31] We are not just robots, but people 'woken up' by the Word.

Now it is the case of Mary that makes clear above all that this faith and obedience must be truly human. For unless that were so, Jesus Christ would not be truly man as well as truly God. The New Man, Jesus, is not created *ex nihilo* but born *ex Maria Virgine*. Barth thus affirms that the virginal conception is an event between God and man, that in 'receiving' and 'being ready', Mary participates as real man. He uses the key phrase that in this event of salvation, 'the female can and must be there, be there for God, if God for his part wishes to work on man and for man.'[32] All this is truly human faith, and yet it is also somehow called into being by God. Barth shows his difficulty when he modifies his key phrase four pages later, and says that '*through the Holy Spirit* it becomes *really* possible for man to be there and to be free for God'.[33] If Barth were suggesting (as he sometimes comes close to doing) that it is only the man recreated by grace who can be reckoned as being 'really' human in the sense of being human *at all*, then it would not be possible to speak of an incarnation in our history, in what Barth himself calls 'the time and history of the sinful creature.' [34]

So we seem to be in an impasse. Barth denies that Mary cooperates with God in salvation, even in the sense of being open for the Word. Yet her receptivity is a really human act, and later Barth admits that such faith is creative. Perhaps we can begin to find a way through if we ask why Barth is so unhappy with the Catholic notion of prevenient grace. He opposes, we recall, the idea that God endowed Mary with grace before she heard the Word of promise, so that she was able to respond to it herself,[35] and had her own desire to give birth to the Son. Barth believes that this would infringe God's sole activity in salvation, because he thinks that such prevenient grace would be a gift quite different from the Word of God in revelation. But suppose we were to think of this prevenient grace precisely *as* the Word of revelation; suppose that God had a'ready been speaking his Word to Mary's heart, in a long story whose beginnings were hidden in the mysterious and inner stirring of the Holy Spirit within her?[36] Then this pre-history of hearing the Word of God would make her open to receive and obey the particular Word of promise about the birth of Jesus.

If this were so for Mary, it would of course be also true for all people. We would have to say that God always speaks his word deep in the heart of every human being, and that this self-giving of God lays the foundation for the moment when a person in conscious faith says 'yes' to the divine word. That is, we would agree with Barth that human beings have no capacity in themselves for knowing God, but we would add that human beings *are* nevertheless open and receptive to God because he is always opening himself to them, and in this constituting their very humanity. Even if they do not realise it, or misunderstand it, God still is offering himself and unveiling himself, so that the point of contact is there. In the phrase of Karl Rahner, the human being is to be defined as a 'hearer of the Word.'[37] Though Barth, of course, rejects the notions of 'general revelation' and a 'point of contact' in human nature, he does not consider the possibility that the 'point' might be nothing less than a personal encounter with the self-revealing God.

Such a perspective would allow us to understand all human beings as cooperating with God in salvation – at least as far as the creative act of their faith is concerned. We can respond to the Word of God in open faith because it is already a hidden part of our life by the gracious gift of God. Why, anyway, should we think of Mary's obedient response as being her *first* act of faith, like a conversion? Actually, when Barth comes to think about sanctification, the process of being made holy by God, he admits that human beings can be fellow-workers with God, and that their works can be judged as 'well done' by God.[38] We can do good works, and even though they are awakened by the Holy Spirit we will still be praised by God for them:

> In accordance with his election and calling and empowering, [man] will do good works as works of faith, conversion and love. They will certainly not praise himself ... But they will have the praise of God and will praise him. [39]

Barth denies that good works gain us any merit, for they are simply a sharing in the good works of God, but they earn the reward of

God's praise. We cannot boast in them ourselves, for as the Apostle says 'let him who wants to glory, glory in the Lord'. But Barth makes the very significant point that we are part of the Communion of Saints, and ought to take note of the way that others have done good works to the glory of God.[40] That, I suggest, certainly applies to Mary.

So, when we come to consider Barth's own thought about the creative character of human faith, the praise of good works and the unity of sanctification with justification, we begin to have a basis for a slightly different view of Mary from the one he proposes. We can, I suggest, honour her as the one who responded to the Word of promise. She points the way for all human beings to say 'amen, let it be so'. Such a response is an active and creative participation in God's own work of salvation, a participation for which he has himself already prepared and taken the initiative in opening himself to us in many hidden ways. It is the story of grace in the life of Mary that requires us to say this, and so she is indeed worthy of honour in the Communion of Saints.

It is in this area of *response* to the initiative of God that the special association of Mary with the figure of *Sophia* (Wisdom) really belongs, and to which we have seen that Barth takes exception. Alasdair Heron, a theologian in the Reformed – and indeed the Barthian – tradition, has made the perceptive comment that after the Arian controversy of the fourth century, it was no longer possible to apply the title 'Wisdom' to the divine Logos (Word). The created wisdom of Proverbs 8:22 could only symbolise being-as-created, and though the humanity of Jesus is certainly the perfect creation, Heron suggests that the word of Mary, 'I am the Lord's servant' may be seen as 'the authentic word of creation itself, true to its nature as created, and responding to its creator.'[41] We must, however, surely add that the title of Wisdom can hardly be applied to *created* beings without implying a *creativity* as part of their nature.

Heron concludes that Mary can at least be seen as a fitting 'expression' of *Sophia Creata*. While we may agree with Heron that this does not make Mary a 'cosmic' figure, we can, I believe, go as far as to speak of an eternal function of Mary and an eternal honour. Once again I wish to suggest that this is in accord with some trends of Barth's own thought (though this development might well surprise him).

3. The eternal motherhood of Mary

I have already pointed out that Barth affirms the ancient title of Mary as 'Mother of God'. This, he rightly says, points in the first place away from Mary herself to Christ.[42] Mary can be said to give birth to God because in the human life of Jesus God has humbled

120

himself and accepted suffering and death. In Barth's view this does not detract from the glory and divinity of the Son of God; God is never more God than when he humbles himself. It is a majestic theme of Barth's theology that God can choose in love to accept all the limits of human life, even to face death. He is free to do this, for God is the God he chooses to be, and it is not for us to say that it is not worthy of him. As Barth affirms, God is free not only to be unconditioned 'but in the absoluteness with which he sets up this fellowship [with his creation], he can and will also be conditioned.'[43] From all eternity, in a primal decree, the Father has chosen that the Son should be made one with a human being, Jesus of Nazareth, and the Son has chosen this destiny with him.[44] Thus man is elected for fellowship with God from all eternity; God opens himself to make room for humanity in his own life when he chooses the man Jesus Christ. Deep in his eternal counsels, he has chosen humanity and thus the way of the Cross.

Now, this surely leads us to say that God must have chosen a woman to be the mother of Christ in the same primordial decree. He does not elect her to be one in *being* with himself as he chooses the man Jesus to be one Person with the eternal Son of God. But she is still chosen. Barth indeed refers to Mary as the very climax of God's election of his people Israel in preparation for the birth of the man Jesus.[45] If Mary is Mother of God at one time in human history, she may surely now carry this title with her into eternity. She always was this in God's intention; she always will bear this dignity, this mark of election within the Communion of Saints. Barth does not say this, but it is consistent with his theological method.

We may look at this from another angle typical of Barth's method in theology. Barth always begins with the revelation of God in the world, and then works his way back into thinking of the eternal being of God. God speaks the truth about himself, interprets himself without deception,[46] and so what we know of God in his revelation must have some correspondence to the eternal nature of God. For example, if God the Son is revealed as humbling himself at the cross, then there is always humility within God.[47] Thus we may say (though Barth does not), that if Christ is the Son of Mary on earth, then something of that relation remains in heaven, though there must be a mystery about what exactly it is. Nevertheless we can surely say that Mary is always Mother of Christ, and in this sense Mother of God. The place of Mary thus keeps alive a testimony to the humanity of Christ. There is humanity in God asserts Barth – what is truly human belongs to him: 'there is no man-less God.'[48] I would add that we shall never forget this if we remember Mary, for Christ is always Son of Mary.

We should, however, separate the idea of the perpetual Motherhood of Mary from an eternal function of mediating between our prayers and Christ, for which she has been celebrated in some Catholic tradition. I would not dare to suggest that anything in Barth's Reformed theology could be pressed into supporting that. Neither, in my own view, can a mediation of Mary be simply extended from the heavenly intercession of Christ and the Spirit portrayed in certain New Testament passages,[49] since this is not a legal pleading with a distant Father on our behalf, but rather a relationship with the Father in which we are invited to participate. Nevertheless, those Protestant thinkers who are unable to follow Catholic tradition about Mary as intercessor, ought perhaps to be prepared to look again at another dimension of her motherhood which they have also often rejected, namely the traditional title 'Mother of the Church' (*Mater Ecclesiae*).[50]

4. Mary and the Church

The ascription 'Mother of the Church' implies, as Barth points out, both that Mary is mother of all believers, and that the Church shares in some way in her motherhood. Barth is unhappy with the title, and in his later years even liked to suggest mischievously that Joseph was a more appropriate 'protector and exemplar of the church' than Mary, since the biblical record presents him so impressively as 'obedient and subservient'.[51] In an interesting passing comment on the dignity of Mary, Barth adds that the function of the Church could hardly be compared with hers anyway. It is worth recording that when Barth met Pope Paul VI in 1966 the Pope embraced him warmly, reminded him of this opinion about Joseph and said he would pray that in his advanced age God would give him deeper insight into the matter.[52]

Barth's preference for Joseph as exemplar is in fact rather odd, even in Barth's own terms. We have seen that he understands Mary as representative of all women in being chosen for the vocation of bearing the incarnate Word, where the male was excluded. This, he suggests, should help to rehabilitate the dignity of women. Now, elsewhere in his *Church Dogmatics*, Barth affirms that it is the woman who fittingly represents the whole Church, rather than the man. The Church is the human community which listens to the Word of God, and while the prime example of the receiver of the Word is Mary, the whole of her sex represents the listener to the divine Word. The Apostle Paul, Barth points out, explicitly compares the woman with the Christian community in drawing the analogy between husband as head of the wife and Christ as the head of the Church:[53] 'The advantage of the wife, her birthright' is that she, not the man, 'attests the reality of the Church as it listens to Christ'. The conclusion seems inevitable that Mary above all is therefore the exemplar for the Church.

Admittedly, Barth ascribes this honour to women because he understands their function in the divine order to be submissive to the initiative and leadership of men; he is wanting to argue that there is no subordination of status in this subordinate function. Not only is the woman equal in honour in her service, but if she is submissive to her husband, then:

> The wife is not less but greater than her husband in the community. She is not the second but the first. In a qualified way she is the community. The husband has no option but to order himself by the wife as she is subordinate in this way.[54]

There is, of course, a smack of masculine patronising about this, as if the woman is to be persuaded against her immediate reactions that all is for the best when she admits the leadership and inspiration of men. A rather different situation is surely implied by Barth's own daring analogy between the relations of the Persons of the Trinity and the relations of man and woman.[55] Though the divine Persons have a difference of function, they also participate in each other's functions through a *perichoresis* (mutual indwelling) of being. Though Barth himself wishes to restrict the analogy at this point,[56] there are rich possibilities here for developing a theology both of gender-difference and gender-sharing.

In our present concern we need not pursue – and destroy – Barth's argument about subordination any further;[57] but we must follow up his insight that Mary represents the listener to the Word. Though Barth declines to do so, it is surely appropriate to call Mary 'Mother of the Church' in the sense that she sets a pattern for belief. Christ himself must, of course, be the archetypal pattern for believers in his human response as Son to God as Father; but Mary is the pattern for fallen human beings in receiving the Word which is Christ. Moreover, Barth underlines the fact that this pattern becomes visible most clearly in a *woman*, who represents all women in the Church. If my argument be accepted that Mary's receptivity is a creative thing, highly active in its own way, then to call Mary 'Mother of the Church' and the Church 'mother' does seem to require (to say the least) a full recognition of the place of women in Christian ministry. All too often an honouring of the Blessed Virgin Mary has been taken as a substitute for the honouring of the ministry of women, rather than as an incentive for it.

In conclusion, my argument throughout this paper has been that there is good basis in Barth's own theology for honouring Mary, and that her response 'let it be so to me' must require us to see her faith (and ours) as playing a more active role in God's work than

Barth admits. In friendly conversation with Barth, the Roman Catholic theologian Hans-Urs von Balthasar once said that 'When I get to heaven, I shall go up to Mary ... and say, "Well done, sister."'[58] This was no trivial remark, for we have it on good authority (Mt 25:21) that the one who does well enters into the joy of the Lord.

Notes

1. Quoted in E. Busch, *Karl Barth: his life from letters and autobiographical texts*, trans J. Bowden (SCM Press, London, 1976), 371.
2. Ibid.
3. Karl Barth, *Church Dogmatics*, Eng Trans ed G.W. Bromiley and T.F. Torrance (T. & T. Clark, Edinburgh, 1936-77) Vol I, part 2, 143. Henceforth this work will be cited as *CD* followed by volume number, part number and page. References to Vol I/1 are to the Second Edition, trans. G.W. Bromiley, 1975.
4. Barth, *CD* I/2, 143; Thomas Aquinas, *Summa Theologiae* III, q 25, art 5.
5. *CD* I/2, 143.
6. Ibid, 138
7. e.g. *CD* I/1, 136.
8. *CD* I/2, 140.
9. *CD* I/1, 407.
10. See e.g. *CD* IV/1, 633-7.
11. *CD* I/2, 191.
12. For the following exposition, see ibid 197-202.
13. Ibid 192.
14. Ibid 193. Barth, however, defines the hidden contribution of the female as a cooperation with the male, showing himself to be limited to 'the power behind the throne' approach.
15. Ibid 194.
16. Ibid 196.
17. Ibid 143.
18. *CD* IV/2, 189.
19. For this paragraph, see *CD* IV/1, 145f.
20. G. Manley Hopkins, 'The May Magnificat', in *The Poems of Gerard Manley Hopkins*, Fourth Edition, ed W.H. Gardner and N.H. Mackenzie (Oxford University Press, London, 1967), 76-8.
21. *CD* I/2, 191.
22. Actually Barth seems to have misunderstood the Catholic tradition of analogy, which is less static than he supposes, and surprisingly close to his own view of an 'analogy of grace' and 'analogy of relations'. See the important discussion by H. Urs von Balthasar, *Karl Barth: Darstellung und Deutung seiner Theologie* (Cologne, 1967), 175ff.
23. 'Confirmation' is used of believer in e.g. *CD* IV/1, 752; of

Mary in e.g. IV/2, 145. 'I discover and confirm myself as the subject intended in [Christ's] being and activity ...' IV/1, 753.

24. See *CD* I/1, 160-2. See further below on 'free' decision.

25. Hans Küng, *Justification: the Doctrine of Karl Barth and Catholic Reflection*, trans T. Collins, E. Tolk & D. Grandskou (Burns & Oates, London, 1964) 251-3, 79-83, 248-9 lays stress on active (and creative) nature of receptivity, while agreeing with Barth's stress on the objective saving act of God. H.Urs von Balthasar makes receptivity a pivotal point of his theology, and sees precisely this as Mary's co-redemptive activity: see Charles Smith, 'Mary in the Theology of Hans-Urs von Balthasar', *One in Christ*, 1986/4, 43f for contemplative activity of Mary.

26. Barth carefully avoids, however, calling it a creative 'act', preferring the phrase 'creative character'.

27. Küng, op cit 67-69. Küng also however maintains that Barth, in line with other Reformed theologians, misunderstands what Catholic theology says about justification as interior transformation; they fail to understand that Catholic tradition tends to include 'sanctification' under 'justification', and to call 'redemption' what Protestants call 'justification' (217, 221-3, 246-8). Thus Catholic thought (and Trent) does not intend to deny the declarative and objective character of God's judgement upon man in the cross and resurrection of Jesus. (Barth suspects, in his letter prefixed to Küng's book, that this is special pleading.) The question arises as to how much Barth *did* see an interior, ontological change in man resulting from justification/sanctification; his stress is undoubtedly upon the pronouncement of justification, and man as *simul peccator* while *simul justus*. Faith is 'taking cognizance' of completed work of Christ. A.B. Come, *An Introduction to Barth's Dogmatics for Preachers* (SCM Press, London, 1963) discusses this, 158ff and concludes that there is a tendency in Barth to make the life of faith an 'empty shell', waiting for the parousia.

28. *CD* IV/2, 501f, IV/1, 95; cf II/2, 756f.

29. *CD* I/1, 454.

30. *CD* IV/1, 633f.

31. Barth attempts to resolve this tension in *CD* I/1, 161f. We have a human choice between yes and no, but the content of this as being good or bad is given by God, 'whereby it is decided who I am in my own decision, and whereby it is decided what my decision really means'. But this seems to be as empty a choice as the 'merely formal capacity' which Barth derides in Brunner: See E. Brunner & Karl Barth, *Natural Theology* trans P. Fraenkel (Bles, London, 1946), 79f, 88ff.

32. *CD* I/2, 195.

33. *CD* I/2, 199. My italics.

34. *CD* I/1, 426.

35. This is the Catholic idea of the 'potential for obedience' of which Barth is critical. For an exposition of this human potential in line with my suggestion here, see Karl Rahner, *Hearers of the Word*, revised by J.B. Metz, trans R. Walls (Sheed and Ward, London, 1969), 157-63.

36. A Roman Catholic might want to trace this back to the immaculate conception, or to see the latter as a *symbol* of the pre-history of revelation. Macquarrie, *Principles of Christian Theology*, Revised Edition (SCM Press, London, 1977), p 398 understands immaculate conception as a symbol for 'common grace' in the people of God, preparing for the receptivity of Mary in the incarnation. See further below (Part III) on the eternal election of Mary.

37. See Rahner, *Hearers of the Word* op cit, 53-68, 111-20; also Karl Rahner, *Foundations of Christian Faith: An Introduction to the Idea of Christianity* trans W.V. Dych (D.L. T., London, 1978), 117-26.

38. *CD* IV/2, 593.

39. *CD* IV/2, 597.

40. *CD* IV/2, 596.

41. Alasdair Heron, 'Predestination and Mary', in *God and Mary: The Way Supplement 25* (*The Way*, London, 1975), p.32.

42. *CD* I/2, 138f.

43. *CD* II/1, 303; cf IV/1, 176, 186f.

44. *CD* II/2, 5f, 101ff, 115ff.

45. *CD* IV/2, 45.

46. *CD* II/1, 657f; I/1, 363, 383.

47. *CD* IV/1, 201.

48. *CD* IV/3,1, 119.

49. Notably Hebrews 4:14-16, Romans 8: 14-15, 26-28.

50. J. Macquarrie, *Principles*, 394 claims that this title is truly ecumenical in appeal. Heron, op cit, also accepts the title, with qualifications from a Reformed standpoint.

51. See for example Barth's letter to B.A. Willems, March 1963, cit. Busch, op cit 467.

52. Busch, op cit 484.

53. Ephesians 5: 22-24. Barth's discussion is in *CD* III/2, 312-16.

54. CD III/2, 314.

55. CD III/1, 189-92; IV/1, 203.

56. CD III/1, 196.

57. For a fuller working out of this theme, see my paper '"Woman's Head is Man": A Doctrinal Reflection upon a Pauline Text.' *The Baptist Quarterly* XXXI (1986), 370-83.

58. Busch, op cit 362.

From an example of virtue to the feminine face of the Church:
Shifts in Marian Perspectives in The Lutheran Tradition.

Revd Professor Sven-Erik Brodd
Swedish Lutheran, Uppsala

This lecture will be divided into three parts. The first one is a survey of the historical development of Mariology and Marian piety in Lutheran tradition. The second will reflect the dialogue between Roman Catholic and Lutheran theology. That will serve as a background for the third part, which will be a draft of principles for a Lutheran concept of Mariology in an ecumenical age.

A. Mary in the history of Lutheranism

1. Retained medieval Mariology in Luther's theology.

In the reformation period, Luther retained most of the medieval Marian theology; not always in a constructive way perhaps, but at least by way of admitting it into the total concept of his Christology.[1]

Thus, Martin Luther confessed that Mary was *delivered from original sin*. It seems, however, that he is not consistent in his view of when this freedom from sin commences. At the time, this was a matter of theological dispute in the Western Church. At first Luther seems to hold the opinion that Mary was preserved from original sin when conceived (*immaculata conceptio*).[2] Later, he obviously taught that Mary was exempt from sin when Jesus was conceived in her body through the initiative of the Holy Spirit. Two years before he died he wrote: '... it was necessary that his mother was a virgin, a young virgin, a holy virgin, who was saved from original sin and purified through the Holy Spirit.' [3]

Luther furthermore stated that she remained *ever-virgin* (*semper virgo*). He preached as late as 1546 that Mary was 'a virgin before conceiving and giving birth, she remained a virgin also at the birth and after it.'[4] This view seems to be a constant in Luther's otherwise rather inconstant theology.[5] The Articles of Schmalkalden, a German Lutheran confession, the *Prima pars, De articulis divinae majestatis IV*, states that Mary is '*pura, sancta semper virgo,*' that is pure, holy ever-virgin.[6]

Mary is holy and according to Luther she is also the *Mother of God* (*Theotokos*). In a treatise 'On Councils and Churches', he writes that 'this council [of Ephesus] did not establish anything new in the faith but defended the ancient faith ... Indeed the article according to which Mary is Mother of God has been in the Church from the beginning.'[7]

Mary was also, according to Luther, the *figure of the Church.* He says that Mary is our Mother as the Church is the Mother of believers.[8]

All those doctrines about Mary may be found in the Swedish Reformers.[9] But already in the sermons of the Swedish archbishop Laurentius Petri, edited 1555, one finds the perspective which later on, in Lutheran homilies, becomes totally predominant: Mary as the ideal believer.

It is evident, then, that the Lutheran reformers included traditional Mariology in their Christological perspective. At the same time, however, they severely criticized the practice of Marian devotions in Church life, appealing in that criticism to the Church fathers.

2. The distinction between Marian dogma and Marian piety in the post-Reformation era

Certainly there was a strong criticism of actual Marian piety in the Reformation period. There was a strong feeling for the exclusiveness of Christ and the uniqueness of the atonement of Christ. Mary as the Queen of Heaven, Marian prayers and the theology stressing Mary's participation in the salvific work of Christ, was rejected.

In the post-reformation period, the traditional theological statements about Mary, related in different ways to Christology and Ecclesiology and positively affirmed, or at least admitted by Luther, began to be disputed among Lutheran theologians. This concerns *semper virgo* and above all Mary's freedom from original sin: It is worthy of note that the development in Lutheranism and Roman Catholicism during the period of Western confessionalism was antithetical. There is obviously a mutual dependence of Marian 'maximalism' in Roman Catholicism and 'minimalism' in Lutheranism.[10] Still, one has to be aware of the fact that, for example, the questions of *immaculata* and *assumptio* were as yet not church-dividing.

The result of this was, of course, a certain tension within the Lutheran tradition gradually taking shape, between what was possible to proclaim on the one hand, and on the other a necessay restraint in order to change or hinder what was regarded as an exaggerated and perverse cult of St Mary. This, too, led to a minimization of dogmatic teaching about Mary and an emphasis on her exemplary role for Christian life, especially for women, not only in the Church but also in society.

3. The minimization of Marian perspectives in Church life in the period of Lutheran orthodoxy

In the 17th century, the time of formation of confessional bodies in Europe, the Lutherans still retained most of the traditional Mariology within the framework of Christology. In the Church of Sweden Hymnal published 1689 and replaced in 1810, the hymns spoke of Mary as the Mother of God (e.g. no. 122), as virgin before, during and after the birth of Christ (e.g. no. 121), and as the pure, holy virgin (e.g. no. 124).

But in the homilies one finds very little of this. Mary is preached as the humble maiden, the example of obedience to God and of perfect piety.

We know, however, from folkloristic studies made in Sweden in the late 19th century and the beginning of the 20th, that Marian prayers and piety had survived in some type of underground existence, becoming ever more perverted due to lack of authoritative teaching in the Church.

Thus, if at least the earliest period of Lutheran tradition yields the picture of a two-tiered Mariology – with doctrinal learning about Mary for the theologians and preaching about Mary as an example for the ordinary church-goers – this picture is complicated by the fact that people, almost three hundred years after the Reformation, could still be found with remnants of Marian piety. It is thus possible to add a third level to the two already mentioned, but it is one which was certainly not in favour among the bishops. It could perhaps be objected that I have overstressed the division of Mariology into two levels. I referred to the Swedish Hymnal; I could also have referred to sermons from the 17th century placing a strong emphasis on the classical Marian dogmas. But I believe my presentaion of the matter is basically correct.

4. Mary as an example of female virtues in rationalistic Lutheran theology

In the latter part of the 18th and the beginning of the 19th centuries Mariology was, of course, in dogmatics still a part of the doctrines about Christ. This must be stressed.

But in practice, Mary was preached in such a moralistic way that she almost lost her role in salvation history. Sermons on Mary stressed purity, virginity and motherhood, but not primarily in relation to Christology, but rather as an example for the life in Church and society of the respectable woman.

The mystical dimensions lost their axiomatic significance for the life of the Church. In relation to Christology, the Virgin Mary was preached merely as a channel, a passive maiden, and her passivity preached made her almost uninteresting.

Scientific biology of the 19th century, being suspicious of miracles, questioned the virgin birth and, most of all, birth from an ever-remaining virgin.

Historical-critical exegesis offered interpretations which, for instance, affirmed earthly brothers of Jesus. History of religion, supported by biblical criticism, found almost nothing left of Mary in the New Testament except influences from other religions in the Middle East. Mariology, even in the New Testament, was thought of as a deviation from the original, Christian religion.

Mary now became the Christian ideal of bourgeois virtues, attached almost exclusively to women.

5. The 19th century dilemma: Romantic Marian revivalism versus Protestant reductionism

The 19th century is even more complex than earlier periods of history in regard to attitudes to Mary in Lutheran tradition.

As a heritage from the Age of Enlightenment, the theologian of the first decades of the 19th century strongly supported the idea of a cooperation between man and the grace of God, the *gratia cooperans*. The Swedish archbishop Johan Olof Wallin says in 1827, 'Because of her eminent virtues, Mary was worthy of God's grace enabling her to give birth to Christ.'[11] This is indeed far from some types of Neo-Lutheranism, to which any type of cooperation is a repudiation of pure grace, of the *sola gratia*.

But one also finds a decisively Protestant attitude, characterized by theological reductionism. This new type of 'Protestantism' is the result of a new concept of the relations between the churches, where 'Protestantism' is looked upon as a principally defined block of churches, theologically the antithesis of 'Catholicism.'

The idea of this type of Protestantism was fanned by the promulgation of *immaculata conceptio* in 1854. Mary is in this connection seen almost as a symbol for Catholicism.

This type of Protestant reductionism neither reckoned with what the Lutheran fathers taught about Mary, nor with the possibility that deduction from what is contained in Holy Scripture might represent truly biblical teaching on Mariology.

When historical-critical exegesis emerged, it was easily integrated with the Protestant principle, and made it possible to exclude traditional statements on Mary also from the New Testament. Theological reductionism was consequently extended also to dogmatics.

At the same time, however, and this is very interesting, one finds a re-evaluation of the Blessed Virgin Mary, not among theologians but among authors, poets, painters and composers of music. It all begins with *Romanticism*, which idealizes both woman and the Middle Ages. In certain circles of Romanticism, there was also a striving for a higher synthesis of Protestantism and Roman Catholicism. Taken together, this led to a fascination with Mary, expressing itself in different forms of music, paintings, sculptures and poetry. At least in Swedish Lutheranism this has continued, and is, I think, the immediate background to what I am now going to say about the situation in the Church of Sweden today.

7. Marian revival in the last decades of the 20th century

In the Church of Sweden today, it is not possible to preach Mary simply in that moralizing perspective which was previously mentioned. It is impossible to appeal to a model of virtue, valid first and foremost for women, in which Mary is humble, obedient, remaining silent in Church and society, unobtrusive, pleasant and domesticated. What, then, would be the alternative?

In 1985, a leading Swedish newspaper announced the return of Mary in the Church of Sweden.[12] There are indeed reasons for that statement. I will give some:

In 1985, *the fourth Sunday in Advent was dedicated to Mary, the Mother of the Lord*. Earlier the Liturgical Year included the traditional Sundays of Visitation, Annunciation and Purification. The motive for this addition of a Marian Sunday was, according to the General Synod, an intention to strengthen the place of Mary in Church life. In reality, of course, the General Synod merely aligned itself with a development already in progress.

The recently (1986) ratified Church of Sweden Hymnal contains *new hymns about Mary*. What actually is taught about Mary in the Hymnal is not always easy to grasp, but at least the Church of Sweden now for the first time has got a version of *Salve Regina*, giving praise to Mary (no. 480), as well as a prayer to her, 'O Mary... teach me to love Him who has passed through death and grave to the Kingdom of light' (no. 481, v.4). The *sacred music* includes all types of Marian themes. The texts are, with few exceptions, either medieval or modern. And this is symptomatic.

In a research report about Marian music, mostly vocal and then performed by church choirs, on the Sunday of Annunciation 1985, in the Church of Sweden, 240 different Marian hymns or versions of hymns were performed, among them about 30 different versions of *Ave Maria* and 10 of *Ave Maris Stella*.[13]

In the Church of Sweden, one also finds *statues and pictures of Mary* in almost every church building. These statues and pictures are both medieval and modern, but hardly one may be found from the times in between.

Here, it is obviously a question of the renewed appreciation of Mary among artists of different kinds that has now reached to the very centre of the Church.

Very much of the return of Mary in the Church of Sweden is emotional. But at the same time, it is a sign of an increasing awareness of the role of women in the Church, a new sense of the mystical dimension and above all, a need for manifestations of the feminine aspects of the Christian faith. Those aspects are relevant to both man and woman and when focused in Mary, they expose the feminine face of the Church.

8. Some concluding remarks on the historical development

When the Lutheran fathers retained so much of the Catholic teaching on Mary, but, as it seems, avoided it in preaching in favour of a decidedly moralistic view of her, they initiated a process that was to lead to a fading consciousness of Mary's place in the history of salvation. Even though almost every statue and picture of Mary and the other saints was preserved in Sweden after the Reformation, and likewise Marian motifs in the Hymnals, she faded from the spiritual life of the Church. When this process had reached its climax, new impulses to Marian piety from outside the boundaries of theology stimulated to a new appreciation of Marian piety and a rethinking of Mariology. Today in the Church of Sweden, this movement has reached right into the liturgy of the Church. But the theologians, in my opinion, still sit on the threshold. Articles and books are, of course, written about certain aspects of Mary, but the only attempt to write a Mariology so far is by a lay member of the Church and Member of Parliament, symptomatically a woman. It is also, typically enough, published by the Church of Sweden Cultural Institute. [14]

B. Mary in the Roman Catholic–Lutheran Dialogue

If it is true what Lutheran theologians say, that the Lutheran Reformation did not intend to play a constitutive but a corrective role, not having the intention to form a new Church but to reform the one Catholic Church in Europe, then the so-called Lutheran Churches are always dependent on their Mother Church, the Roman Catholic. [15]

And if this corrective view is true about the Church, it follows that the Lutheran Reformation did not want to create a new Mariology but to correct the Roman Catholic one.

This, in my opinion, is of vital importance to ecumenical methodology as well as to Mariology. Lutherans ought not only to reiterate the statements of the Reformation, but to investigate their context, in order to expose their relevance today. A principally understood interdependence between Lutheranism and Roman Catholicism implies a common re-evaluation of the whole post-reformation development.

The question then, in the light of the historical outline already presented, is what Lutherans, in relation to Roman Catholic theology, think about Mary today.

1. The lack of ecumenical dialogue about Mary before the Second Vatican Council

Before Vatican II, the question of Mariology had been a source of increasing controversy between Lutherans and Roman Catholics, with few exceptions.[16] Protestant reductionism and Roman Catholic maximalism had dominated the respective traditions. The encyclical *Munificentissimus Deus*, 1.11 1950, promulgating the dogma of the Virgin Mary's translation to heaven, was met with strong opposition among Lutherans, but also from the Orthodox, Anglican and Reformed Churches. This opposition was increased in 1954, when Pius XII declared the Marian year and inaugurated the new liturgical feast, Mary Queen of Heaven.

The different Marian revelations, for instance at Lourdes 1858, Knock 1879 and Fatima 1917, also had made Protestants suspicious. World War I had brought liberal theology to an end in Lutheranism, even if it was to have a certain impact afterwards. In the 1930's, 1940's, and in the 1950's, there was a new Lutheran understanding of its heritage, in Sweden usually combined with a High Church view on the sacraments, the liturgy, and the ordained ministry.[17] There was also a new appreciation of the unique character of the Swedish Reformation. But still, with few exceptions, the Protestant attitude to Mary remained unaltered. What should be observed in the development in Lutheranism, beginning in the 1950's, is a certain interest in Luther's view on Mary.[18] Almost simultaneously occurs in Roman Catholic theology a new interest in Mariology as an ecumenical problem and sometimes as an opportunity. [19]

2. General prerequisites for Roman Catholic–Lutheran Dialogue on Mary

Personally, I think there are three bases for today's new possibilities of fruitful dialogue between Lutheran and Roman Catholic theology:

The first basis is the fact that Vatican II did not promulgate a specific document on Mary, but integrated Mariology into the Constitution on the Church, *Lumen gentium*.[20]

The second is the rediscovery among Lutheran theologians of the interdependency of biblical interpretation and tradition. A very good example of this is the excellent work, *Mary in the New Testament*, written jointly by scholars from different Christian traditions. Here, Roman Catholic and Lutheran scholars are found in agreement on what was said about Mary in the New Testament. The result of the investigation is well exemplified by the position these scholars take on the question of the virginal conception: ... 'one's attitude towards Church tradition on the matter would probably be the decisive force in determining one's view whether the virginal conception is a *theologoumenon* or a literal fact.'[21]

The last basis is the need for doing theology, attested by the rise of new theologies, some of them unrelated in origin to traditional confessional theology, for instance liberation theologies and – especially relevant for Mariology – the feminist theologies.[22]

And so, as a consequence primarily of the three factors mentioned, the climate of discussion changed during the 1970's. The methodology of controversial theology was relinquished, and new methods in search for convergence were inaugurated.

3. Some reflections on the present theological dialogue on Mary

I shall now very briefly relate the principal contents of the German dialogue between Roman Catholic and Lutheran theology on Mary, mainly from a Lutheran point of view, making some comments as a Swedish theologian.

On Christology

There seems to be a consensus about Mariology being a part of Christology. Earlier differences, originating on the one hand in liberal Protestant theology and on the other in tendencies in Roman Catholic theology, not always admitted by Roman Catholic theologians, to emancipate Mariology from Christology, are now in principle overcome. So there is really no need to go into the classical Marian dogmas on *semper virgo*, *Theotokos* and so on.[23] There is, however, one exception, and that is the *conceptio immaculata* or Mary's freedom from original sin. This doctrine is not discussed in a Christological context, but in the framework of a critique of tendencies to parallel Jesus and Mary.[24]

This reflects an attitude in Protestantism but does not contribute to the understanding of theological statements on Christ as God and Mary's Son, on Christ as man but without sin.

On grace and justification

In a Lutheran–Roman Catholic dialogue one must, of course, cope with the question of Mariology in the framework of the main confessional article in Lutheranism, *justification by faith*. But Lutheran theology traditionally, I am sorry to say, proceeds from a number of deductive principles, above all 'by grace alone' (*sola gratia*) and 'by faith alone' (*sola fide*). The question in Mariology, as in every other dogmatical *locus* of Lutheran theology, is then how to combine these different principles. It is not at all clear how to interpret Mary's role in light of the Lutheran teaching on justification by faith. It should not be, if one considers that the Lutheran tradition is ambiguous.[25] We have seen for instance that Luther held Mary to be delivered from original sin, and that a 19th century Swedish arch-bishop confessed Mary to be cooperating with grace.

We are now faced with the remarkable situation, that Roman Catholic theologians claim the Marian dogmas of *immaculata conceptio* and *assumptio* to be expressions of the Lutheran theology of *sola gratia*,[26] while Lutheran theologians question that.[27] The basic problem seems to be that when Roman Catholics talk about Mary's role in salvation, it is in terms of a realization and application of the unique, salvific work of Christ alone (*solus Christus*) while Lutherans interpret this as if they meant to give Mary a complementary function in relation to Christ.[28]

On Mary and the Bible

The question of Mary in the Bible is also dealt with in the Lutheran–Roman Catholic dialogue. Here we meet again one of those Lutheran deductive principles, the 'Bible alone' (*sola scriptura*).[29] The concept is known, of course, like everything in the theology of the Reformers, since ancient times. Thus St Thomas Aquinas taught, *Sola canonica Scriptura est regula fidei* – The only norm of faith is the canonical Scriptures.[30]

What then is the Mariological difference between Lutherans and Roman Catholics according to *sola scriptura*?

Personally, I think the difference today originates from Lutheran biblicism combined with historical-critical exegesis.

Lutheran theologians stand today before the great task of re-examining the role of this type of exegesis in theology, and especially the role it has played in the origin of reductive Marian theology.

On the Church

It seems as if Lutherans have certain difficulties with Mary as the *typos* of the Church. On the one hand, it is possible to regard Mary as the prototype of the Church,[31] as long as both are seen under the perspective of openness to God, service, obedience and communion with God in Christ.[32] On the other hand, there are hesitations and even objections against giving Mary and the Church, (admitting that Mariology and Ecclesiology are mutually dependent), an active role in the ongoing salvific work of Christ. This seems too much like threatening the unique character of Christ's role in the Church and in the history of salvation. Therefore, every idea of cooperation in (*cooperatrix*) or mediation of salvation (*mediatrix*) by the Church or by Mary, is rejected.[33] This in spite of Roman Catholic assurances that Mary and the Church belong to the historical realization of salvation, and that every form of cooperation and mediation is by Christ and through Christ.[34]

On Marian piety

Mary is the model of the ideal believer, and as such, she ought, according to German Lutheranism, to be venerated.[35] As a part of creation, however, she can never be an object of prayers. The Roman Catholic distinction between different forms of prayer is not accepted. But it is still possible to integrate Mary in the liturgy, in hymns, art, and music, and even to mention her in the prayers. [36]

Outcome of the Lutheran–Roman Catholic Dialogue

A fundamentally corrective or regulative, i.e. non-constitutive Lutheran theology today, dealing with Mariology, proceeds from the basis of Roman Catholic theology.[37] The weakness of this method is that the corrective principle, whether explicitly used or not, seems to restrain Lutheran theologians from constructive theological reflection on Mariology. The situation provokes attitudes of Lutheran criticism and Roman Catholic self-defence. But, if my interpretation of the Lutheran position is correct, there are also tendencies today to submit the Lutheran history of Mariology and Marian piety to new considerations. This means new possibilities for constructive Mariological work.

C. A Lutheran re-construction of Mariology in an ecumenical context.

Some preliminary remarks

Taking into account the historical development and the, in principle, corrective self-understanding of Lutheranism, I would like to suggest a tripartite division of the Marian perspective for Lutheran tradition in an ecumenical age:

1.Mary's significance for Christology

It is obvious that Lutheranism has to reconsider its confessional development in view of its original standpoint on, for example, the teaching about *semper virgo*. The problems about that dogma are not separative between the Roman Catholic and Lutheran churches, but constitute a common theological task and should be dealt with as such.

2. Mary's integral function in Ecclesiology

Mary is the prototype of the Church, but also the mirror in which the Church is able to see its own ideal image. It is in relation to Christology that one can regard Mary as the *prototype of the Church*, which gives birth to the love of God in baptism, remains ever-virgin, never falters in her perfect love for Christ, partakes in Christ's own life, being united with Christ through the blood circulating in both bodies at the same time, the Eucharist. This perspective proceeds from Christology, because it depends on the understanding of the relation between Christ and Mary.

But Mary is also the *image of the Church*, that is, she provides models for the life of the believers, the *communio sanctorum*, that *communio* to which she herself belonged in her earthly life and still belongs in her heavenly. As we know from history, Mary as image had traditionally been related almost exclusively to women. It is my opinion that this is an outcome of an individualistic trend in Mariology. If Mary is the image of the Church, she should not be used as a mirror reflecting the perfect woman, but should represent the pattern for Christian life. This, firstly for the Church as a whole, then for the congregation, and lastly for the individual Christian (man or woman).

In both cases, as prototype and as image, Mary is the feminine face of the Church, integrating theology and Christian life in an organic, living perspective. In this particular aspect, this feminine face corresponds to the masculine face of the Church represented by the concept Body of Christ. In neither case can the concepts be a source of identification for man or woman alone, but for the Church as a whole.

3. Mary in the devotional and liturgical life of the Church

It is of course necessary for theological models to be applicable to the piety of the Church. Thus the teaching on Mary has to find its place in devotion and liturgy. It is easy to demonstrate that Lutheran theology and spirituality has attached much less importance to Mary than the reformers did.

Personally, I take it for granted that the Lutheran Churches pray *with* Mary and all the saints. In the Swedish Mass we pray together with all the saints of all times. We sing together, giving her praise in the new Church of Sweden Hymnal. More controversial is, of course, the question of Marian prayers. As we have seen, however, there are a tremendous lot of Marian prayers in Church music performed by choirs in the ordinary services of the Church of Sweden.

In conclusion, I would like to stress that Mariology is an opportunity to integrate Christology and Ecclesiology in Church life. History teaches us that this is possible only when Marian piety is allowed to find concrete expressions.

Notes

1. Schimmelpfennig, R. *Die Geschichte der Marienverehrung im deutschen Protestantismus*, (Paderborn 1952); Tappolet, W. (Hrsg) *Das Marienlob der Reformatoren* (Tübingen 1962); Düfel, H. *Luthers Stellung zur Marienverehrung* (Göttingen 1968); Hennig, H.J. 'Die Lehre von der Mutter Gottes in den evangeliöch-lutherischen Bekenntnisschriften und bei den lutherischen Vätern', *Una Sancta* 16 (Meitingen 1961), 55-80; Meinhold, P. 'Die Marienverehrung im Verständnis der Reformatoren des 16. Jahrhunderts', *Saeculum. Jahrbuch für Universalgeschichte* 32 (1981), 43-58.

2. Luther, Martin. *Praelectio in librum Judicum*, 1516, WA 4:559; Id, *Festpostille*, 1527, WA 17, 11:409; Id, *Vorlesung über das Hohelied*, 1530/1531, WA 31, 11:689. About Luther's shift of opinion, see Tappolet, W. *Des Marienlob der Reformatoren*, (Tübingen 1962), 29-32.

3. Luther, Martin. *Vom Schem Hamphoras und vom Geschlecht Christi*, 1543, WA 53:640: 'Darumb war es not, das seine mutter were eine Jungfraw, Eine junge Jungfraw, Ein heilge Jungfraw, die von der Erbsunde erlöset und gereiniget durch den heligen Geist...'; Id, *Enarratio capitis noni Esaiae* [1543/44], 1546, WA 40, 111:680.

4. Luther, Martin. [*Predigten des Jahres* 1546] WA 51:167.

5. Tappolet 1962 49-54; Schimmelpfennig 1952, 13ff; Düfel 1968, 154f.

6. In the German edition is written 'rein, heilig Jungfrau', *Die Bekenntnisschriften der evangelisch-lutherischen Kirche*. Hrsg vom Deutschen evangelischen Kirchenausschuss...1930, 414 (5. Aufl. 1963).

7. Luther, Martin. *Von den Konziliis und Kirchen*, 1539, WA 50:59lf. See also Id, *Das Magnificat vorteutschet und auslegt*, 1521, WA 7:545; Id, *Predigt am Epiphaniastage*...1532, WA 36:60; Id, *Betbuchlein* [Das Ave Maria], WA 10,11:407.

8. Luther, Martin. *Kirchenpostille*, 1522, WA 10, 1:405f; Id, [*Predigten des Jahres* 1523], WA 11:144, 219, 224; Id, [*Wochenpredigten über Joh. 16.20*, 1528/29], WA 28:402; Id, [*Predigten des Jahres* 1529], WA 29:655,656.

9. Brodd, S-E. 'Predikan om Jungfru Maria i Laurentius Petris postillor', in: *Predikohistoriska perspektiv. Studier tillägnade Åke Andrén, utg A. Härdelin*, (Stockholm 1982), 183-212, Summary: Mary in the Books of Homilies by Laurentius Petri, the Archbishop of Swedish Reformation.

10. Delius, W. *Geschichte der Marienverehrung* (Basel 1963); Söll. G, *Mariologie*, (Freiburg 1978) Handbuch der Dogmengeschichte, hrsg von M Schmaus u.a., Bd 3:4).

11. Brodd, S-E. 'En ren och hjertlig fromhet.' Kring den moraliska

mariabilden hos Johan Olof Wallin, in: Håkan Möller (utg), J.O. Wallin. *Uppsatser och studier*, Uppsala 1989 [in print].

12. Jonasson, C. 'Renässans för Jungfru Maria', *Svenska Dagbladet* 4, April 1985.

13. Brodd, Birgitta/Brodd, S-E. *Mariamusik*. En undersökning av det kyrkomusikaliska utbudet i Svenska kyrkan Jungfru Marie Bebådelsedag 1983 - Särskilt mariamusiken (Stockholm 1984) (Religionssociologiska institutet. Forskningsrapport 1984: 1-2).

14. Aner, K. *Jungfru Maria, Herrens moder* (Stockholm 1983) (Svenska Kyrkans Kulturinstitut. Dialogserien 24).

15. Kinder, E. 'Kann man von einem "lutherischen Kirchenbegriff" sprechen?', *Theologische Literaturzeitung* 81 (1956), 385-398;Id, Evangelische Katholizität. 'Ueber den ökumenischen Horizont in Luthers Kirchenauffassung', *Luther* 35 (1964), 25-33; Brodd, S-E. Evangelisk Katolicitet. '*Ett studium av innehåll och funktion under 1800- och 1900-talen*', (Lund 1982), 263-318 (Bibliotheca Theologiae Practicae 39).

16. Völker, M. 'Mariendogma und Marienverehrung im dialog der Kirchenseit 1950', *Ökumenische Rundschau* 30 (1981), 1-20; Bibliography in Köster, H.M. 'Die Rolle der Bibel im Marienverständnis des neueren deutschen Protestantismus', in: *Heilige Schrift und Maria, hrsg von Deutschen Arbeitsgemeinschaft für Mariologie* (Essen 1963), 245-254 (*Mariologische Studien Bd 2*).

17. See e.g. Giertz, B. *Kristi Kyrka* (Stockholm 1939), German transl. *Die Kirche Christi*, Gottingen 1951 (5. ed Göttingen 1955).

18. Delius, W. 'Luther und die Marienverehrung', *Theologische Literaturzeitung* 79 (1954) 409-414; Künneth, F.W. 'Luthers Marienzeugnis und das theologische Ringen des Gegenwart', *Zeitwende* 35 (1964), 661-647; Preuss. H.D. *Maria bei Luther*, Gütersloh 1954 (Schriften des Vereins für Refomationsgeschichte 127); et al.

19. Sartory, Th. 'Maria und die getrennten Brüder', *Una Sancta* 1954, 10-20; Bea, A. 'Mariologie, marianische Frommigkeit und ökumenischer Geist', *Stimmen der Zeit* 174 (1963/64), 321-330; Congar, Y. M-J. 'Marie et l'Eglise chez les protestants', in: *Chrétiens en dialogue* (Paris 1964), 490-518.

20. Mühlen, H. 'Neuorientierung und Krise der Mariologie in den Aussagen des Vaticanum II', *Catholica* 29 (1966), 1953.

21. Ed R. E. Brown, K.P. Donfired, J. A. Fitzmyer, J. Reumann, *Mary in the New Testament: A Collaborative Assessment by Protestant and Catholic Scholars* (Philadelphia/New York 1978), 292; On the role of the bible in modern Lutheran understanding of Mary, see Köster, H.M. op cit, 166-244.

22. Radford Ruether, R. *The Feminine Face of the Church* (Philadel-

phia, 1977); Mulck, Ch. *Maria - die geheime Göttin im Christentum* (Stuttgart/Zürich 1987) Beinert, W. *Maria in der feministischen Theologie*, Catholica (Paderborn 1988), 1-26; Halkes, C. J. M. 'Eine "andere" Maria', *Una Sancta* 32 (1977), 3233-337; Schöpsdau, W. *Mariologie üns Feminismus*, Bensheim 1985 (Bensheimer Heft 64).

23. 'Maria - Evangelische Fragen und Gesichtspunkte. Eine Einladung zum Gespräch. Für den Catholica-Arbeitskreis der Vereinigten Evangelisch-Lutherischen Kirche Deutschlands (VELKD) und des Deutschen Nationalkommitees (DNK0 des Lutherischen Weltbundes (LWB) heausgegeben vom Lutherischen Kirchenamt der VELKD', *Una Sancta* 37 (1982), 184-201, cite Maria/VELK.

24. Maria/VELKD, op cit, 190ff, 195

25. Volk, G. ' Maria zwischen den Konfessionen', *Una Sancta* 36 (Meitingen 1981), 76-88.

26. Fries, H. Maria – Stein des Anstosses oder Chance für die Ökumene?', *Stimmen der Zeit* 207 (1989), 158-170.

27. Maria/VELK op cit, 195.

28. Mary/VELKD op cit, 197f.

29. Maria/VELKD op cit, 185, 198.

30. Persson, P. E. *Sacra doctrina. En studie till förhållandet mellan ratio och revelatio i Thomas av Aquinos theologi* (Lund 1957), 54 (Studia theologica Lundensia 15).

31. Maria/VELKD op cit, 186.

32. Maria/VELKD op cit, 198, 195.

33. Maria/VELKD op cit, 194f.

34. Fries, op cit, 168.

35. Maria/VELKD op cit, 194ff.

36. Maria/VELKD op cit, 196ff.

37. It seems as if the two main obstacles in the Roman Catholic–Lutheran dialogue should be the Papal ministry and Mariology. Scheffczyk, L. 'Petrus und Maria. Hindernisse oder Helfer auf dem Weg zur Einheit?', *Catholica* 34 (1980), 62-75; Heft, J.L. 'Papal Infallibility and the Marian dogmas', *One in Christ* 18, 1982-4, 309-40.

The language of divine motherhood in the liturgy of the Church

The legitimacy and limits of inclusive language in Christian devotion

Revd Norman Wallwork
Methodist, Keswick, Cumbria

'Rule One' in the missionary proclamation and celebration of twentieth century Christian faith includes the necessity of taking on board the cultural and sub-cultural languages and thought forms of those whose Christian formation we treasure. As William Gowland never tires of telling the Methodist people in Britain, you cannot redeem what you do not understand. Thus, despite all opposition, the Church represents its dogmas and doctrines in the light of the best contemporary philosophy and science and it re-translates its biblical and liturgical texts from one language into another and encourages the use of modern language texts alongside more traditional forms. Even within, say, the eucharistic rites of the English speaking Catholic hierarchies, there are already such sub-cultural rites as Mass forms for use with school children.

Already the Catholic Bishops' Conference of England and Wales has, since November 1986, approved the omission of 'men' in the Words of Institution over the chalice in all eucharistic prayers. These now read, 'It will be shed for you and for all'. Already the House of Bishops of the General Synod of the Church of England has commended the widely used *Lent, Holy Week, Easter: Services and Prayers*[1] in which 'neighbour' replaces 'fellow men' in the act of penitence. In 1984 the British Methodist Conference authorised some thirty instances in the Methodist Service Book where words of the masculine gender had a meaning that embraced both male and female and a list of alternatives was suggested.

The Church of England Liturgical Commission has recently published a major report *Making Women Visible: the Use of Inclusive Language*[2] in which alternatives are suggested for whole phrases which may appear to be exclusive as well as recurring words such as 'man, men, mankind, sons, brothers, and fathers'. Perhaps one of the more interesting for this ecumenical society is the suggestion in the eucharistic prayers that instead of 'giving him to be born as man and to die upon the cross' the text might read 'giving him to be born of Mary and to die upon the cross'.

Complete liturgical texts which have already been published

include the inclusive language version of the *Grail Psalms*[3] and a number of recent denominational service books in the United States.[4]

There is of course a profound linguistic battle to be fought over inclusive language outside as well as inside the Church, but on the grounds of sensitivity to one highly significant sub-culture the Church's pastoral love and wisdom may convince its liturgists to concede the issue with regard to collective nouns and personal pronouns. This pastoral concession, however, is a far cry from the other major aspect of inclusive language which concerns the names and nouns we apply to the Godhead.

On this issue I wish to suggest that pastoral love is not the only consideration. Providing it is said clearly that tenderness and motherliness are not exclusively feminine characteristics, there is much to be said in favour of the Church including in its liturgies scripture sentences, biblical passages and collects which highlight both the feminine and motherly images of all three persons of the Trinity and scriptural narrative which celebrates the place of women in salvation history. Indeed, the Church needs to over-compensate in this direction for its sparse provision of such material in the past. Outside of scripture the Church needs also to provide from the fathers and mothers of the faith those rich veins of spirituality such as Anselm of Bec and Mother Julian of Norwich which rejoice so obviously in the mother image in the relationship between Christ and the individual Christian.[5]

There are two areas, however, in which I believe much more is at stake in the names, nouns and pronouns applied to the Godhead than the great seven last tragic words of the Church – we've never done it this way before! The first serious mistake is the rash way in which the Divine Wisdom has been scattered over many modern liturgical texts. It is fair to claim the feminine pronoun for Wisdom but it is far from clear, in the last analysis, to which person of the Godhead Wisdom refers. I think I would want to claim that Wisdom belongs to the poetic element in the liturgy – as in the first of the Great Advent Antiphons and as in one of Charles Wesley's finest hymns which not only applies the feminine pronoun but proclaims that 'Wisdom, and Christ, and Heaven are one'.[6] In this context it is not legitimate, as a general rule, I suggest, to address the whole of the eucharistic prayer to Eternal Wisdom as is the case with all the experimental canons in the otherwise excellent liturgical texts and collects in Janet Morley's *All Desires Known*.[7] Indeed the stunningly beautiful preface in the canons of Janet Morley's collection will only work if the whole of the eucharistic prayer is addressed to the second person of the Trinity. This method of offering the eucharistic prayer, though not without ancient precedent, cuts at the root of the

Church's understanding of its prayer and sacrifice of praise being offered to the Father, through the Son, in the Holy Spirit.

In a similar vein are the very beautiful doxologies from the liturgical writings of Jim Cotter, such as:

The blessing of God, Life-Giver, Pain-Bearer, Love-Maker
be with us now and always.

Or the slightly more traditional:

Great praise and everlasting glory be to God,
Sustainer, Redeemer, Sanctifier. [8]

In trying to eliminate the nouns 'Father' and 'Son' from the traditional trinitarian formula, attributes or functions are objectified, or if this is not the case then at least we must say that the ultimate metaphors of scripture are being avoided. When the Church says that Christ is the Son of the Father it is saying something very different from describing the Father as Creator and the Son as Saviour. The word 'Redeemer' is a good example of this somewhat dangerous terrain for it can be applied either to the first or the second person of the Trinity.

Even if the Church concedes that all language about God is provisional I think we have to assert that some metaphors are more penultimate than others. This, of course, brings us to the nub of the matter before us which is the plea that the Church addresses the first person of the Trinity as 'Mother' quite interchangeably with 'Father'. The issue is by no means helped by dismissing the argument out of hand. For, in the ultimacy which lies beyond the bounds of the Church militant here upon earth, God may not be 'Our Father'; but in the only provisionality which we have been given 'Father' is the primary metaphor which Jesus gave both to the Church and to the world. Such a reactionary thought must not go unmitigated for it behoves us all to rediscover the lost femininity and maternity in the Fatherhood of God which is as present as his masculinity and his paternity. Nor must we neglect the femininity and the maternity which belong to our relationship with the other two persons of the holy Trinity.

But there is a further argument against the liturgical addressing of God as Father *and Mother*. Boldly stated it is this. The Divine Motherhood in the universality of Christian spirituality belongs to another who is not divine, namely the *Theotokos*, the Mother of God.

Luther, Zwingli, Bullinger and practically all the Uncle Tom Cobleys of the Reformation never shrank from calling Mary 'Mother of God' and in one Max Thurian, who even yet, may be claimed as a child of the Reformation, we read:

The dogma of the divine motherhood of Mary is part of seeing clearly the humanity of Christ. To call Mary the 'Mother of God' is to recognize that God became incarnate so completely and so really in our human flesh that He had a truly human mother and was a truly human son in a human family. [9]

The essence of the argument is this. The Church's shout of praise to Mary as her mother and the Church's cry of intercession that she will pray for us as surely and more surely than any other Christian mother on earth or in heaven means that rightly or wrongly the universal Church has already given the titles, honours, and praise of divine motherhood to the mother of God incarnate. When the plea goes up that the titles and attributes of motherhood be given to God the Father in the public and private devotion of Christians the Church must declare that the titles, honours and praise are already spoken for. Mary is not the divine Mother by virtue of the adjective but by virtue of the noun and in the Christian dispensation of two thousand years of the Church's spirituality the noun cannot in practice, even if it can in theory, be transferred to another without mind-boggling liturgical and devotional confusion.

Notes

1. *Lent, Holy Week, Easter: Services and Prayers* (Church Publishing House, London, 1986).
2. *Making Women Visible: The Use of Inclusive Language with ASB* (Church Publishing House, London, 1989).
3. *The Grail Psalms: An Inclusive Language Version* (Collins, London, 1986).
4. *The United Methodist Service Book* (Nashville, 1988).
5. Ed. Alan E. Lewis, *The Motherhood of God* (The Saint Andrew Press, Edinburgh, 1984).
6. *Methodist Hymn Book* No.360, London, 1933.
7. Ed. Janet Morley, *All Desires Known* (Movement for the Ordination of Women, London, 1988).
8. Jim Cotter, *Prayer at Night: A Book for the Darkness* (London and Exeter, 1983).
9. Max Thurian, *Mary: Mother of the Lord and Figure of the Church* (Faith Press, London, 1963).

Mary in the Apostolic Church: work in progress

Rev Eamon R. Carroll O.Carm.
Roman Catholic, Loyola University, Chicago

I have taken my assigned topic to mean recent studies on our Lady in the New Testament, with particular attention to writings of ecumenical provenance. It is to be noted, however, that there has been no successor to the pace-setting *Mary in the New Testament: A Collaborative Assessment by Protestant and Roman Catholic Scholars* (London: Chapman; Philadelphia: Fortress; New York: Paulist, 1978). It was edited by two Catholics and two Lutherans, Raymond E. Brown, SS (who continues to write on the nativity materials) and the Jesuit exegete Joseph A. Fitzmyer, and the Lutherans Karl P. Donfried and John Reumann. In addition there were eight other contributors: two Catholics, two Lutherans, two Anglicans, one the New Testament expert, British-born Reginald Horace Fuller, now retired from teaching, and Elaine Pagels, known for the study of Christian gnosticism, also a German Reformed (Paul J. Achtemeier) and the Presbyterian J.L. Martyn.

Mary in the New Testament grew out of the Lutheran-Roman Catholic consultations in the United States, by virtually the same authors who had put together the 1973 *Peter in the New Testament.* The writers worked as a team 'to see whether, as a group of scholars from different Church backgrounds, we could agree upon a presentation of the New Testament data about Mary.' With the exception of a single chapter the investigation was on New Testament materials. Within these limits, the Scriptures alone in historical-critical analysis, the book was a remarkable success. One example of their consensus was the consideration of the story of the 'true kinsmen,' also known as 'the coming of the mother and the brethren,' in all three synoptics (Mark 3, Matthew 12, Luke 8). In contrast especially to St Mark the Lukan version praises the relatives of Jesus, particularly his mother as the one who before all others hears the word of God and does it.

Another point of considerable importance for New Testament light on our Lady was also made in this book; I attribute it particularly to the input of R.H. Fuller: it is 'canonical criticism', which is the evaluation of the added possible meanings gained by once-separate books when they are joined into the one canonical collection we call the Bible. As far as Mary is concerned, 'canonical criticism' affects not only the relationship between the testaments, but also internal relationships in the New Testament. 'For example, we shall see how difficult it is to determine whether a Mary/Eve parallelism was in the mind of the Fourth Evangelist when he described the mother of Jesus at Cana (2:1-11) and at the foot of the cross (19: 25-27), or in the mind of the author of the Book of Revelation when he described the struggle between the mother of the messianic child and the dragon who was the ancient serpent (Revelation 12). But when John and Revelation are put in the same canon, a catalytic action may occur so that the two women are brought together and the parallelism to Eve becomes more probable' (pp 30/1). Overall, *Mary in the New Testament* was a record of common discovery of lines of biblical development that show Mary as the disciple *par excellence* and as the Virgin. The authors give this testimony: 'From the New Testament pictures of her we learned afresh something of what faith and discipleship ought to mean within the family of God' (p 6).

I interject here, although it's not the particular subject of this paper, notice of a book just published, by George H. Tavard, AA, stimulated by his membership in the United States Lutheran-Roman Catholic dialogue: *The Forthbringer of God: St Bonaventure on the Virgin Mary* (Franciscan Herald Press, Chicago, 1989). The dialogue has been engaged since February, 1984, in studying problems between Roman Catholic and Lutheran traditions on 'the subject of the Virgin Mary, her relationship to Christ, her position in God's plan of salvation, her place in Christian dogma and piety.' Tavard did a paper for the Feb, 1986, meeting, comparing Bonaventure and Duns Scotus on the theology of the Virgin Mary; that led him to deeper studies of Bonaventure. He says in his foreword: Bonaventure, who, unlike Scotus by whom he has been overshadowed, did not accept the Immaculate Conception. He offers us an earlier perspective on the Virgin Mary, antecedent to the formulation of the later Marian dogmas. He writes: 'The ecumenical question, prominent today, urges all Christian believers to review the points where Catholics and Protestants have differed with both eagerness and sincerity. The place of the Virgin Mary in doctrine and piety is one of these points of divergence.' For Tavard 'the heart of Bonaventurian Mariology is to be found in his recurrent reflections on the Annunciation.' His closing paragraph in the foreword reads: 'I dedicate this work generally, in an ecumenical spirit, to all the Christian believers who feel respect and veneration for the Virgin Mary, Mother of Christ, Forthbringer of God, and who share with St Bonaventure and the older theologians their disagreement with the modern Catholic doctrine of the Immaculate Conception.'

Recent writings about Mary in the New Testament
The October 1988 *Biblical Theology Bulletin* had the article, 'Da-

vid: A Model for Mary in Luke,' by the Old Testament professor at the Lutheran Gettysburg Seminary, Dr Richard N. Nelson. Taking a cue from the 1940 study by Eric Burrows, SJ, on Luke's 'imitative historiography,' Dr Nelson describes the verbal links between David and Mary. Both are models of faith; the Mother of Jesus is the 'faithful disciple,' the 'new David.' Some of Nelson's comparisons are fairly common knowledge; others refreshingly new. The similarity St Luke intended between chapter one and chapter seven of 2 Samuel extends to a number of statements. David says, 'Who am I, Lord God, and who are the members of my house, that you have brought me to this point?' (2 Sam 7, 18) and Mary's words in Luke 1, 34: 'How can this be...' David's courtly language, 'Lord God, you have also spoken of the house of your servant for a long time to come' (2 Sam 7, 19) is reflected in Mary's 'Behold the servant of the Lord.' David said: 'And now, Lord God, confirm for all time the prophecy you have made concerning your servant and his house, and do as you have promised' (2 Sam 7, 25) with the echo in Mary's consent, 'Let it be done to me as you say.'

Our Lady's 'my spirit finds joy in God my Saviour' had antecedents in Hannah's hymn 'My heart exults in the Lord, my horn is exalted in my God' (1 Sam 2, 1), but also in David's prayer, 'Your name will be for ever great, when men say, The Lord of Hosts is God of Israel'(2 Sam 7:26). For Simeon's sword in St Luke Dr Nelson traces a reference again to the life of David, this time 2 Sam 12, 10: 'Now therefore the sword shall never depart from your house, because you have despised me... and taken the wife of Uriah to be your wife.'

There are many differences among scripture scholars, differences that transcend confessional lines, as, happily, their agreements likewise transcend membership of various Christian Churches and groups. Apart from certain inescapable requirements of consistency I do not feel obligated to follow any single biblical expert closely, so that some of the findings here reported are more of a potpourri than an intricately interwoven interpretative pattern. With respect to differences, especially for the infancy accounts, where divergent exegetical views are sometimes rather sharply expressed, I put before you the wise words of the late Neal Flanagan, brilliant Servite New Testament scholar, who died November, 1985, and with whom I shared a lecture platform in San Francisco shortly before his death. On that occasion Fr Flanagan, himself a partisan of the historical-critical style of exegesis, like Raymond E. Brown, and in contrast to René Laurentin, had this to say: '...notwithstanding a scholarly insistence on the symbolic, rather than historical presentation of Mary in the gospels, a few persistent questions remain. Why was it precisely

Mary who was chosen as the symbol of discipleship, of attentive hearer, as doer of the word, as the blessed among women? Why not someone else? Why is it Mary who appears at the foot of the Cross as representative of Christ's spiritual family? Why not someone else?...What cords of tradition tie the symbolic and artistic presentations of both Luke and John to the historical personage of our Lady? Is it even possible to imagine that Luke paints his annunciation scene, as John his Calvary scene, without knowing through historical information that Mary was a worthy, if not superworthy, model? Primarily symbolic though they be, these paintings of Mary must flow from historical memories that established her as a primary Christian model.' (Neal M. Flanagan, OSM, 'Mary of Nazareth: Lady for All Seasons,' in *Listening: Journal of Religion and Culture* 22 (Autumn, 1987) 175). 'The difficulty, the frustrating difficulty, is that we can no longer reach back through the symbol to the historical elements which made the symbol plausible'; (this sentence is not in the *Listening* article but in the same article in an earlier publication, 'Mary of Nazareth: Woman for All Seasons,' in *Marianum* 48 (1986) 160).

Apropos of the ongoing debate between Fr R.E. Brown, on the symbolic side, and Fr R. Laurentin, on the historical side, Fr Flanagan noted that they defend their respective positions with untiring energy, adding these peaceful words: 'I do expect all of us, no matter what side we are on at the moment, to listen to the other side with openness and respect. Only thus can theology and mariology advance' (*Listening*, p.179). I would say that the ESBVM puts that good advice into practice.

In his latest study on Cana, A. Feuillet reported that a recent book on John's Gospel by D. Mollat calls attention to a truly historical source for the narrative of Cana, noting how shortly before (two days prior, with Cana on the third day) there is a remarkable example of pinning down an unforgettable event concerning the first followers of Jesus, two former disciples of the Baptist, one of whom was Andrew. 'They spent the day with him; it was about the tenth hour' (1, 39). M.-J. Lagrange saw similar realism there. (A. Feuillet, 'Les espousailles du Messie: La Mère de Jésus et l'Eglise dans le quatrième Evangile,' in *Revue thomiste* 86 (1986) 536-75).

Within recent years two new books on Mary of the Bible have appeared in English, and a third, with much biblical material, in both English and French. The title that came out in both languages was by the French-Canadian Jean Pierre Prévost, SMM. The English edition, *Mother of Jesus* (Novalis, Ottawa, 1987) has a foreword by Dr Joseph McLelland of McGill University, Montreal, who described himself as a Protestant, Church not indicated. He writes, 'I commend this book to all, particularly those Protestants who still suffer from the "silent conspiracy" among us which caused us to drop Mary from our theological concerns. We have missed so much.' Fr Prévost alludes to Catholic movements on the fringe of the Second Vatican Council, groups with the commendable goal of restoring Marian devotion, yet ignoring the council's directions and subsequent teachings, such as Pope Paul VI's and the present Holy Father's. Rather 'they have chosen to nourish themselves almost exclusively from private revelations... should Marian teaching be limited to these kinds of experiences?'

The two full-length books were Walter T. Brennan, OSM, *The Sacred Memory of Mary* (Paulist Press, Mahwah, NJ, 1988) and Joseph X. Grassi, *Mary, Mother and Disciple* (M. Glazier, Wilmington, DE, 1988). Fr Brennan presented the Scriptures and the liturgy as the primary ways by which the Church preserves the memory of Mary and teaches us joyfully to reverence her memory. When we recount the memory of Mary in word and worship we share in a present mystery. 'We encounter Jesus and Mary today, praying with them, following Jesus, living the faith of Mary.' The first Christians recalled the memory of Jesus in word and worship, strikingly aware of his continuing presence. The Gospels contain the earliest written record of the sacred memory of Jesus and his Mother. The concern of the Church, then as now, was not only to *know about* our Lord and our Lady, but to *know* them with a personal living and loving knowledge. The Church is called to remember Mary always within its memory of Jesus Lord and Saviour, as the Holy Spirit, the Spirit of Jesus, brings to remembrance all that God has revealed to us in Christ. Jesus promised us at the Last Supper, 'The counsellor, the Holy Spirit, whom the Father will send in my name, he will teach you all things, and bring to your remembrance all that I have said to you' (John 14, 26).

From the Church's intimate memory of Mary we derive the lessons of prayer and faith. When we reflect on the Gospel prayers of the Blessed Virgin – the short prayer which was her reply to Gabriel, 'Be it done unto me according to thy word,' and the longer prayer of the Magnificat, we gain an insight more intimate even than private letters. We are invited to share the holy Virgin's sentiments before the Lord, to say to her, 'Dear Mother Mary, pour the love of your heart into our hearts.'

Like the sacred memory of Jesus, of which it is an inseparable part, the sacred memory of Mary goes beyond simple recollection. The Church's consciousness of the Mother of Jesus far surpasses ordinary biographical detail. Rather than limiting themselves to a normal biography, the evangelists depict our Lady 'writ large.' We might say the Gospels describe the Blessed Virgin in large block letters, something like the way artists have depicted her as the 'mantle-Virgin,' a towering motherly figure gathering all manner of men and women, girls and boys, under her protecting cloak. The late Hans Urs von Balthasar (d. 1988) wrote in *Mary for Today* (1987): The wonderful truth is that 'no one, whether he or she wants to or not, fails to find room under her cloak...her Son by his suffering has chosen all people to be his brothers and sisters.'

What are some of the further treasures preserved for us by the sacred Gospel memory of Mary? J.X. Grassi in *Mary, Mother and Disciple* shows that for the early Church, and still today, in our age of neo-gnosticism, Mary testifies to the human reality of Jesus – his birth, his mission, his suffering and death, his resurrection, and his continued presence to the Church through his Spirit and through the eucharistic breaking of bread. For St Luke the Mother of Jesus is the key witness to her Son's genuine humanity. Nothing was more typically human than that the Christ-child be wrapped in swaddling clothes, twice mentioned by the evangelist, and linked to the sign of the manger. A manger was for feeding animals; the baby that is placed there, for want of room in the inn, will become the nourishment of his people in the eucharist; he will be the bread of life.

'Bread' is a central theme in St Luke's gospel: Jesus eats with every sort of person – tax collectors, sinners, even Pharisees. Banquets are common elements in our Lord's preaching and parables, as his career moves towards the climax of the Last Supper. After the resurrection St Luke tells the story of Jesus walking as a stranger with the two dejected disciples returning to Emmaus, and how after their hearts were burning when he explained the Scriptures to them they finally recognized him in the breaking of bread.

As we know from our human experience, and mothers know best of all, mothers have the gift of remembering. St Luke sees the Mother of Jesus as enriching the church by her memories. He tells us that the Virgin Mary was deeply troubled by the angelic salutation and wondered what Gabriel's words might mean. She did not hold back from asking in faith: 'How can this be?' When the shepherds arrived in haste, after the angel had told them the good news that the Messiah had been born in David's town of Bethlehem and that they would find him in a manger wrapped in swaddling clothes, St Luke tells us that Mary treasured all these things and reflected on them in her heart.

When the 12-year old Jesus was lost and found in the temple, his words were strange and disturbing: 'Why did you search for me? Did you not know that I had to be in my Father's house?' Mary and Joseph, we read, 'did not grasp what he said to them.' Jesus returned obediently to Nazareth, where he progressed steadily in wisdom and age and grace before God and men. What of his Mother? St Luke says that she too progressed in wisdom and grace, for she kept all these things in memory. She kept all the words about her Son and by her Son, pondering them in her heart. This was no ordinary memory on Mary's part; she remembered and compared, turning over in her heart, mulling over, ruminating over what she had heard and seen and experienced, seeking ever more profound appreciation and acceptance of God's mysterious and merciful ways.

Far more is meant in the Lukan infancy Gospel than tender recollections of the childhood of Jesus. His opening chapters are irradiated by the light of Easter. Mary bears witness to the hidden divine plan behind her Son's suffering and death. She exemplifies the advice the angels gave the women on Easter morning: 'Remember how he told you, while he was still in Galilee, that the Son of man must be delivered into the hands of sinful men, and be crucified and on the third day rise.' (Luke 24, 6-7).

On January 1, 1987, in announcing the recent Marian Year (1987/8) Pope John Paul II called Mary 'the memory of the Church.' Mary as remembering Mother is guarantor also of the Eucharist in the Gospel of John. St John attaches great value to the signs of Jesus, from Cana to Calvary. The mid-point sign was the multiplication of loaves to feed the hungry crowd. Our Lord promised the Eucharist in his discourse on the bread of life, which followed the sign of the loaves, the five loaves multiplied so generously that twelve baskets were left over. On that occasion Jesus explained: 'I am the living bread which came down from heaven; if any one eats of this bread, he will live forever; and the bread which I shall give for the life of the world is my flesh...he who eats my flesh and drinks my blood has eternal life and I will raise him up on the last day.' (ch.6). In the Johannine signs (he always calls the Lord's miracles 'signs') Cana is first and Calvary last. Both occur in the time setting of Passover; John records the Passover as occurring just after the Cana wedding. The sign of Cana is the weak water turned into rich wine at the wedding feast. The sign of Calvary includes the words of Jesus to his Mother, 'Woman, behold your son,' followed by his death and the flow of blood and water from his pierced side. At both Cana and Calvary the Mother of Jesus is present: on both occasions Jesus addresses her not as 'mother,' but as 'woman,' recalling the original woman, the first Eve, mother of all the living, but now Mary, new Eve, mother of those who live again in Christ.

At Cana Mary teaches obedience to Jesus, telling the waiters to do whatever her Son orders. At his command they fill the jars with water, and take a sample to the chief steward, who discovers it has become splendid vintage wine, a wonderful wedding gift, almost beyond measure in quantity and quality. But only the obedient waiters know whence it has come. When Mary said to Jesus, 'They have no wine,' he replied, 'My hour has not yet come.' For St John the hour of Jesus is the hour of triumph on the cross. Mary represents the Church as a concerned mother asking for the new wine of the Spirit, to be poured out exuberantly when the Risen Jesus sends the Holy Spirit. In its deepest sense the holy Virgin's advice to the Cana waiters is her advice also to us: if we obey the teachings of Jesus, understood in the light of his death and resurrection, we too will be filled with the Spirit.

The study by A. Feuillet referred to above (he has been writing on this subject for several decades) points out that in effect Jesus, guest at the wedding, usurped the groom's customary role of serving the best wine, and indeed did so at the end of the banquet. Jesus the messianic bridegroom is the new host, looking to the royal nuptials to be consummated on Calvary. His Mother Mary plays a new Eve role in the scene, with her Son the new Adam.

Aristide Serra: on the Mary of the Gospels

The Italian Servite Aristide Serra published in 1987 *Maria secondo il Vangelo* (Queriniana, Brescia ; expressing for a wider audience two earlier studies: *Contributi dell'antica letteratura giudaica per l'esegesi di Gv 2, 1– 12 e 19, 25– 27* (Roma, 1977) and *Sapienza e contemplazione di Maria secondo Lc 2, 19. 51b* (Roma, 1982)). Four chapters are on the Magnificat. Here are some of Serra's observations: Luke wrote between the years 70 and 90, and his gospel is suffused with Easter faith and paschal joy. What he says about the Mother of Jesus radiates that same orientation.

'Nothing is impossible to God,' were the words of Gabriel, repeating the promise the Lord had made to Abraham and Sara (Gen 18). Through the story of the Annunciation, with Mary as the hearer and singer, Luke sets the stage for the paschal hymn of triumph which is the Magnificat. The canticle of our Lady is Mary's Easter meditation; she was there in the Upper Room, part of the company devoted to the apostolic teaching and to the fellowship and to the breaking of bread and to prayer. In Luke's infancy narrative Mary received the shepherds, treasuring their words and pondering them in her heart. Now in Luke's second book (the Acts of the Apostles) the Mother of the Risen Lord is attentive still to the pastors, who are now the apostles. Jerome, Gregory the Great, Ambrose, Origen and Bede of England all favoured this interpretation.

The Old Testament hymns of joy are gathered and surpassed in Mary's hymn. There are many expressions of joy in the Gospels, e.g., the praise of the people who heard the good news from Jesus the Saviour, who, himself filled with joy through the Holy Spirit, praised the Father for his revelation to little children. How often the joy of the people burst forth into praise, as at the cure of a paralytic (Matthew 9: 2-8), after a healing session in which the mute spoke, the lame walked and the blind saw (Matthew 15, 31). At the Last Supper we hear Jesus say, 'I have told you this so that my joy may be in you and that your joy may be complete' (John 15, 11); again 'I say these things while I am still in the world so that they may have the full measure of my joy within them' (17, 13). In the conclusion of her canticle, 'He has come to the help of his servant Israel, for he has remembered his promise of mercy, the promise he made to our fathers, to Abraham and his children for ever,' Mary reaches the depths of God's heart. God called his people of old to be consoled and to be consolers (Exodus 34, 6). Out of mercy he called them from Egypt in the Exodus. The God of mercy forgave their sins, both the community's when they worshipped the golden calf, and individuals' sins, as with his servant David.

With all Israel Mary knew herself to be touched by divine mercy. Her sensitivity to simple human need, as with the failing wine at Cana, illustrated her ability to show mercy in turn. Jesus said of himself: 'The Son of Man came to seek and to save what was lost' (Luke 19, 10). The Gospel tells how he landed from a boat in what they thought would be a solitary place – he had been so extended in his charity, so many people coming and going, his hungry apostles did not have a chance to eat – to find awaiting him a huge crowd, and according to Mark he had compassion on them, because they were like sheep without a shepherd. The Church, according to 1 Peter 2, 10, is the people of God that has obtained mercy. Correspondingly, the Church's task, as St Paul instructs the Corinthians, is to share St Paul's own joy, and where correction is required, even punishment, it must be followed by forgiveness: 'You ought to forgive and comfort him, so that he will not be overwhelmed by excessive sorrow. I urge you, therefore, to reaffirm your love for him... all in the sight of Christ' (2 Cor, 2: 1-11).

Serra devotes a chapter to the sign of the swaddling clothes. They signify infant weakness, helplessness, but more is surely intended, for in Lukan hindsight the glory announced to the shepherds must be the paschal glory of the Lord, here in contrast to the fragile newborn. In still another fascinating chapter Fr Serra elaborates on the word 'house,' in St Matthew's line, 'On coming to the house, they saw the child with his mother Mary and they bowed down and worshipped him.' In the Hebrew Bible 'house' can stand for the people, the community as well as for the kingdom. New Testament authors show a similar usage, applying the term to the Church, as Paul advises Timothy (1 Timothy 3, 15) on 'how people ought to conduct themselves in God's household, which is the church of the living God, the pillar and foundation of the truth.' Ephesians (2, 19) is similar: 'You are no longer foreigners and aliens, but fellow-citizens with God's people and members of God's household.' How does St Matthew use the word 'house' otherwise? It occurs in the parable of the kingdom (city or household) divided against itself (11, 25), again at the disappointing visit of Jesus to Nazareth, where his own townsfolk took offence at him and he was moved to say, 'Only in his home town and in his own house is a prophet without honour.'

There are Easter likenesses to the visit of the Magi: at the end of Matthew 28, 16-20, the eleven meet Jesus on the mountain in Galilee, as he had instructed them, and as the women at the tomb had been told by the interpreting angel, 'Go quickly and tell his disciples: he has risen from the dead and is going ahead of you into Galilee. There you will see him.' As the star went before the Wise Men, so the Risen Christ goes before his disciples; like the Magi, they find him and adore him, literally, 'they saw and worshipped,' as in the nativity chapter, 'On coming to the house they saw the child with his mother Mary and they bowed down and worshipped him.' The gentile visitors from the East did not find the Saviour in hostile Jerusalem, but in (safe) Bethlehem. Similarly, for Matthew, his disciples were reunited with their Master not in hateful Jerusalem but in humble Galilee. Serra extended his investigation into the Fathers as well: e.g., Irenaeus noted that the house into which Matthew brought the Magi is the house of Jacob, now the house of Christ. Origen and John Chrysostom saw it as the house of spiritual bread. It became common to identify the house with the Church, as in St Bonaventure and other medieval authors.

It has been possible only to scratch the surface of the rich materials on Mary in the Bible, books, articles, parts of books, by many Christian writers, some with deliberate ecumenical intent, but all useful for a better understanding of the true role of our Lady, and hence contributing to the cause of Christian unity, and the ultimate unity for which Christ prayed. Fr Raymond E. Brown got out in time for Christmas (1988) a small book *A Coming Christ in Advent* (Liturgical Press, Collegeville, MN), articles gathered from recent issues of periodicals, among them one on the Annunciation, the Visitation and the Magnificat. Such guides as New Testament Abstracts call attention to articles on our Lady, in many languages.

A feminist consideration

Some feminist writers have taken up the topic of the Mother of Jesus in the Scriptures. An adequate assessment of such studies would require a separate extended paper. One article of unusual value, however, has come to my notice, reasoned and written in a calm and convincing manner: Janice Capel Anderson of the University of Idaho published in the *Journal of Religion* (from the divinity school of the University of Chicago), April, 1987, 'Mary's Difference: Gender and Patriarchy in the Birth Narratives.' In much feminist writing the word 'patriarchal' is taken pejoratively rather than neutrally, and so is the word 'androcentric.' However I cannot report on this interesting article without using the author's terms, neither approving nor refuting! Anderson begins by noting the patriarchal and androcentric character of the Bible, even more in the Old Testament. Having stated that, under the heading of 'the significance of gender as a primary analytic category'; and granting that such studies as R.E. Brown's monumental *The Birth of the Messiah* and the collaborative volume *Mary in the New Testament* do recognize issues raised by modern women in emphasizing Mary as 'the first Christian believer, disciple, and model of faith for men and women,' J.C. Anderson offers from the standpoint of feminist exegesis a further interpretation and enrichment of New Testament criticism. She gives her reason: 'that a feminist rhetorical literary analysis provides a new perspective on the Matthaean and Lukan birth narratives.'

The birth narratives of Matthew and Luke arise out of a patriarchal/androcentric background: both associate female gender with the realm of birth and nurture. Both reflect 'a male cultural view that this realm is a source of female power and difference, controlled by patriarchal social, political, religious, and economic arrangements.' Yet the versions of male ideology in Matthew and Luke are 'not stable'; there are tensions, for Mary differs from all previous scriptural models. 'Thus, the Matthaean and Lukan birth narratives simultaneously project and undermine a male ideology and its associated patriarchal institutions.'

Matthew's genealogy is patrilineal, characterizing Jesus as the Christ, son of Abraham and son of David. Yet the patriarchal pattern is broken by the inclusion of five women, four rather unlikely choices, Tamar, Rahab, Ruth, Bathsheba, and then Mary herself. Various interpretations are suggested by scholars for Matthew's choice of what some have called these 'shady ladies.' They were sinners, one interpretation runs, and Jesus came to save sinners; another view is that they represent the gentile world; a third is that however scandalous their production of an heir may have been, all served as instruments of the Holy Spirit in moving forward God's plan and continuing the messianic line. Anderson emphasizes this third (positive) aspect: it is God who has the power of life and death and control of the womb, and this ties in well with Mary's virginal conception, conferring an affirmative value to the antecedent women in the genealogy. 'The women foreshadow Mary and prepare the implied reader for a woman's irregular production of the Messiah outside of ordinary patriarchal norms yet within God's overarching plans and an overall patriarchal framework.'

Unlike the other four women Mary is unique in virginally conceiving the promised one, the Messiah. In the Lukan birth narratives a similar pattern unfolds – Luke both celebrates and domesticates female difference. 'Mary's powerful role as mother is contained in a patriarchal package.' 'The very "otherness" of Mary and of Jesus' conception make Mary and Zechariah apt foils for one another....' The contrasting comparisons bring out well that Mary is the 'first Christian disciple.'

'If the reader focuses on God's control, rather than that of male or female, husband or wife, then patriarchal control is undermined.' In other words, God is not being viewed as the ultimate patriarch, as a cosmic symbol of male dominance, but rather as an image that undermines male dominance by devaluing human fatherhood and patriarchal institutions. 'Mary is blessed not only as the mother of the male Messiah, but also as a representative of all in Israel, male and female, who rely on God's redemption.' Anderson's final sentence runs: 'The way in which the birth narratives project and undermine versions of a male ideology of female difference also helps us to understand how women in later church history achieved partial independence and exercised leadership through vows of virginity despite pervasive androcentrism and patriarchy.' (Daniel J.Harrington, SJ, cites an earlier article of J.C. Anderson as an example of feminist hermeneutics in his article, 'New and Old in New Testament Interpretation: the Many Faces of Matthew 1:18-25,' in *New Theology Review* 2 (February, 1989) 46).

Conclusion

At this conference copies were available of the February, 1989, number of *The Month*, with the article by Edward Yarnold, SJ, of our ESBVM, 'Mary and the Work of ARCIC.' Fr Yarnold lists the eight points of agreement in the second statement on Authority from ARCIC I. The eight points follow the statement that the two Churches 'can agree in much of the truth that these two dogmas [the Immaculate Conception and the Assumption] are designed to affirm.' They are:

1. Whatever is stated concerning Mary must not obscure the unique mediatorship of her Son. 2. What is affirmed concerning her is 'inseparably linked with the doctrines of Christ and of the Church.' 3. Her 'grace and unique vocation' is recognised. 4. Both Churches include Marian feasts in their calendars, 'according her honour in the communion of saints.' 5. She was 'prepared by divine

156

grace to be the mother of our Redeemer.' 6. She was herself 're-deemed and received into glory.' 7. Mary is a 'model of holiness, obedience and faith for all Christians.' 8. 'It is possible to regard her as a prophetic figure of the Church.'

Marianum (48(1986) 167-9) published as a tribute to Neal Flanagan, OSM, (d 22 Nov. 1985) his 'A Marian Creed.' Here are its high points, remarkably similar to the ARCIC agreement: 1. I believe that Mary's *Fiat* initiated the Christian era and was the prototype of all Christian faith, of the Christian's openness to God. 2. I believe that Mary's *Fiat* inserted her intimately into Christ's salvific work. Mother of Yahweh's suffering servant, she, too, was swept into the pain and suffering and glory that comes with self-giving love. 3. I believe that Mary's openness to God was paralleled by her openness to the needs of her neighbour: to those of Elizabeth, to those of the newlyweds, to those of the crucified Christ, to those of the nascent church. 4. I believe that Mary's continuous Yes to her God and her neighbour is the existential expression of her radical sinlessness as expressed in the doctrine of the Immaculate Conception. 5. I believe that Mary's assumption, like Christ's resurrection, is our proof and our hope that love is truly stronger than death. 6. I believe that Mary, as mother of Christ, was largely responsible for his personality traits and for the creation of his home environment. 7. I believe that Mary is not simply a model or an ideal, but a living person of exquisite loveliness. This I believe, Lord; help my unbelief! Amen

NOTES ON CONTRIBUTORS

ALBERIC STACPOOLE OSB is a monk of Ampleforth Abbey (Yorkshire) and is at present Senior Tutor at St Benet's Hall, Oxford. He has published numerous articles in the area of ecumenism, theology and ministry; and has edited *Mary's place in Christian dialogue* (1982), *Mary in Christian tradition* (1984), and *Mary and the Churches* (1986) for the ESBVM. Since 1980 he has been General Secretary of ESBVM which involved planning four international congresses.

CANON JOHN MCHUGH is the English member of the Pontifical Biblical Commission. Till recently he has lectured on the New Testament at Ushaw College and in the University of Durham. He is the author of *The Mother of Jesus in the New Testament* (1978). He is a regular contributor to ESBVM.

DR KALLISTOS WARE is a monk of Patmos, Bishop of Diokleia, a Fellow of Pembroke College and Spalding Lecturer in Eastern Orthodox Studies at Oxford. At the Dublin Congress (1984) he provided a paper on 'The sanctity and glory of the Mother of God', which provoked a debate that issued in a dialogue at the Chichester Congress (1986) between himself for the East and Dr Edward Yarnold SJ speaking for the Western Church tradition.

REBECCA WEAVER, an American patristic scholar, is a professor at the Union Theological Seminary, Richmond, Virginia. She has given papers to the USA branch of our Society.

ARCHIMANDRITE EPHREM, otherwise Rev Christopher Lash, is an Orthodox monk living at a monastery near Whitby in North Yorkshire. Brother of Professor Nicholas Lash of Cambridge, he was a member of the Department of Theology at Newcastle University until some years ago when he took early retirement to become a full-time monk. It is of interest that both brothers were educated by the monks of Downside.

IAN DAVIE is a master at Ampleforth College, specialising in English literature. He is the author of *Piers Prodigal and Other Poems; A theology of speech; Roman Pentecost; Jesus Putusha* (Lindisfarne Press, USA); and *Angkor Apparent* (1988). In his writings he combines two interests, literature and theology.

SISTER LUTGART GOVAERT has long been secretary to the International Centre of Newman Friends. Her doctoral dissertation was upon Newman's mariology. She is a member of The Work, whose English abode is Newman's College, Littlemore, Oxford, and is presently assigned to the Christian Information Centre, Jerusalem.

PAUL S. FIDDES, an Oxford doctor in theology and Principal of Regent's Park College, the Baptist Permanent Private Hall in Oxford, founded for the Baptist ministry at home and abroad, has specialised in the work of Karl Barth as a University tutor in doctrine. His early writings include books on the Old Testament, charismatic renewal, leadership in the local church. His recent books are *The Creative Suffering of God* (1988), *Past Event and Present Salvation* (1989), and *Freedom and Limit: a dialogue between Christian doctrine and modern literature* (1991?).

SVEN-ERIK BRODD, a Swedish Lutheran minister, is a professor of theology in the University of Uppsala. His doctoral dissertation was on 'The concept of evangelical catholicity'(Lund 1982). He has recently become Doctor of Studies in the International Study Department of the Church of Sweden. He has written several books and contributed to books and periodicals.

NORMAN WALLWORK, a Methodist minister and Superintendent of the Keswick and Cockermouth Methodist Circuit, is the Society's Liturgical Secretary and virtual author of our developing Ecumenical Office, used for prayer in the Society and beyond it. His most recent ESBVM Pamphlet is entitled, 'The Cult of Our Lady in the Presbyterian and Catholic ministeries of W. E. Orchard' (January 1990).

EAMON R. CARROLL O.CARM., a professor of theology at Loyola University of Chicago. His areas of expertise are the New Testament and Mariology. He regularly contributes up-dating surveys of recent Mariology to *Marian Studies*. His contribution to the Chichester Congress was 'The New Testament Charisms of the Blessed Virgin Mary', *Mary and the Churches*, 98-106.